The Chicano

Clio Books/Pacific Historical Review Series

Norris Hundley, jr., Editor

The American Indian

The Chicano

The Asian American

The Chicano

Edited by Norris Hundley, jr.
Introduction by Matt Meier and Feliciano Rivera
Foreword by Miguel León-Portilla

Essays by

Félix D. Almaráz, Jr.

Rodolfo Acuña

Neil Betten

Arthur F. Corwin

Abraham Hoffman

Carey McWilliams

Raymond A. Mohl

Richard L. Nostrand

William B. Taylor

Elliott West

Charles Wollenberg

87

CLIO BOOKS

AMERICAN BIBLIOGRAPHICAL CENTER—CLIO PRESS

SANTA BARBARA

OXFORD

ISBN paperbound Edition 0–87436–213–X
ISBN Hardcover Edition 0–87436–212–1

The articles by Arthur M. Corwin, Carey McWilliams, Félix D. Almaráz, Jr., William B. Taylor and Elliot West, Charles Wollenberg, Neil Betten and Raymond A. Mohl, and Richard L. Nostrand appeared previously in the *Pacific Historical Review*, Vol. XLII, No. 3 (August, 1973). The article by Abraham Hoffman appeared in the *Pacific Historical Review*, Vol. XLII, No. 2 (May, 1973) and that by Rodolfo Acuña appeared in the *Pacific Historical Review*, Vol. XLIII, No. 1 (February, 1974). The Foreword by Miguel León-Portilla and the Introduction by Matt Meier and Feliciano Rivera are published herein for the first time.

Library of Congress Cataloging in Publication Data

Hundley, Norris, jr., comp.
   The Chicano.

   (Clio Books/*Pacific Historical Review* series)
   Chiefly essays from the *Pacific Historical Review*,
v. 42, No. 2–3, 1973.
   Includes index.
   1. Mexican Americans—History—Addresses, essays,
lectures. I. *The Pacific Historical Review.* II. Title.
E184.M5H86   973'.004'6872   75–2354
ISBN 0–87436–212–1
ISBN 0–87436–213–x pbk.

American Bibliographical Center—Clio Press, Inc.
2040 Alameda Padre Serra
Santa Barbara, California

European Bibliographical Center—Clio Press
Woodside House, Hinksey Hill
Oxford OX1 5BE, England

Composed in linotype Baskerville by
Kimberly Press Inc., Goleta, Calif.
Printed and bound by R. R. Donnelley
and Sons Co., Crawfordsville, Ind.
Cover design: Jack Swartz.

Contents

Foreword

Iɴ ᴏᴄᴛᴏʙᴇʀ 1973, the Fourth International Congress on Mexican Studies was held in Santa Barbara, California. There, and for the first time in that series of professional and friendly encounters, Chicano historians as well as a large group of Chicano students were active participants.

The subjects discussed in that meeting—as had been the case in previous conferences held in Monterrey, Nuevo León, 1949; Austin, Texas, 1958; and Oaxtepec, Morelos, 1969—dealt with different aspects of research in Mexican culture and history. Although in Santa Barbara the accent was put on contemporary Mexico, there was also a session dedicated to an appraisal of pre-Hispanic, colonial, and nineteenth-century developments. Questions concerning periodization, regional history, institutional history, education, work, law, and U.S.-Mexican relations received particular attention. In addition, there was a session devoted to Chicano history and culture, which generated great interest among all present and which obviously accounted for the keen participation of Chicano students and professors.

The meeting offered an opportunity to discuss how Mexico's past and present related to Chicano cultural realities. Naturally and inevitably, the perspectives of the Mexicans, Anglos, and Chicanos often differed sharply. Even when using similar or identical sources of information, they adopted views reflecting the indelible coloring of feelings and presuppositions derived from unidentical cultural backgrounds.

Within such context, I presented a paper entitled "History from the Inside and Outside." My point was to describe two specific kinds of historical research, different though not necessarily contradictory nor mutually exclusive. By historical research from the inside, I meant the practice of delving into the history of one's own country or culture. On the other hand, when an alien—even one who is sympathetic toward and familiar with a country or group foreign to him—writes the history of another culture, he will inevitably produce something different, something written from the outside. By this, I do not mean to suggest that historical research from the inside is necessarily the best approach. Obviously, both native and alien scholars may produce very poor or extremely significant works. But writing history from the inside is a valuable—indeed, a necessary—approach. It is one that has been advocated time and again by people throughout the world. Thus were born the myths of origin, oral traditions, and the early historical writings. In contrast to this, writing the history of a people or nation to which the researcher does not belong has not always flourished. To write history from the outside is something most often accomplished by members of a country or community economically more prosperous and powerful than those people being studied.

The above observation can be easily illustrated. There are, for instance, numerous European and North American publications dealing with the history of Latin American and African countries, but the reverse is rare and in many cases simply nonexistent. Among nations or groups described as underdeveloped or belonging to a cultural minority or to the so-called Third World, this situation has produced fear—fear that others will view them only as the powerful outsiders depict them. This reaction has, in turn, encouraged such peoples to do serious research from the inside and to develop a self-image of their own.

In some respects, I believe that this is what has been happening in the Chicano community. Until the last two decades, most of what was written about that community's history and culture came from the outside. Chicanos were generally deprived of the possibility to do research about themselves and were often forced to accept what others said about them. Their situation could not be compared with that of most other groups or nations in which serious, if limited, historical research had been done from the inside.

Chicano consciousness of the need and meaning of history is by now a well-known fact. This explains the uninterrupted flow of publications dealing with the Chicano, past and present. Many of these new books and papers are still being produced by people from the outside, but others, in increasing numbers and sometimes of varying quality, are being written by Chicanos. All serious contributions from both groups are welcome, for as I have already emphasized, history written from the inside and outside should not be considered as necessarily in collision. Different perspectives will provide opportunities for thoughtful exchange and allow scholars to profit from one another's contributions. Even more, the day will arrive when Chicano historians—doing research now from the outside—will make important observations about Anglo and Mexican national cultures.

The book for which this foreword is written attempts a rapprochement by bringing together significant contributions from the outside and inside. The reprinting in book form of these essays, which originally appeared in several issues of the *Pacific Historical Review*, is an excellent idea. If the Anglo perspectives are more represented here, it is simply a reflection of the fact that there are still not so many Chicanos writing their history. Even so, the presence of the excellent papers of such professional Chicano historians as Rodolfo Acuña and Felíx D. Almaráz, Jr., implies an open recognition of the vital importance of history written from the inside.

For Chicano history to come fully of age, major hurdles must be overcome. First, a larger number of well-trained Chicano historians and other social scientists are needed. Also necessary is a guide to relevant source materials in both United States and Mexican archives. The cataloging and microfilming of documents, the producing of indexes of publications—books, pamphlets, and periodicals in Spanish and English—of value to Chicano history should not be postponed since the danger of irreparable loss exists for many such materials.

The papers included in this book confirm these needs—especially when their authors acknowledge that much remains to be done on the basis of sources that may become available in the future. Success will require the participation of many colleagues—Chicanos, Mexicans, Anglos, and, in fact, scholars from other parts of the world. All of them—whether they do their research from the inside or outside—will possess a common goal: achievement of a deeper understanding of the rich and enduring values in the history and culture of that large minority group whose heritage and destiny are forever linked to the heritages and destinies of the United States and Mexico.

MIGUEL LEÓN-PORTILLA

National University of Mexico

The Chicano

Introduction

THE UPSURGE OF INTEREST in Chicano studies has not only generated a higher level of scholarly inquiry about Mexican Americans, it has also given birth to a new school of ethnic historians. Some critics—journalists, professional writers, historians, and Chicano activists—have complained that until recently Chicano history was consciously suppressed and that contributions by Chicanos were deliberately ignored by publishers. Though there are wide gaps in Chicano historiography, these critics seem to overlook the pioneering work of such scholars as Carlos Castañeda, George I. Sánchez, Manuel Gamio, Paul Taylor, and Ernesto Galarza. The critics also mistake omission for deliberate suppression. For decades scholarly research on the Chicano was done primarily by anthropologists and sociologists whose work often lacked a historical perspective and reflected greater interest in examining in detail the deficiencies of Chicanos than in identifying the imperfections of a society which denied its minorities equality of opportunity in employment, education, and politics.

Though historians have generally been latecomers in discovering the Chicano, some important works of a historical nature began appearing as early as the beginning of this century. Government-funded studies, masters' theses, doctoral dissertations, and articles in professional and popular journals examined various aspects of the Chicano experience. Unfortunately, most of this material has never been adequately cataloged or made readily available to the public in published form. Indeed, even today there is no major depository in the United States for Chicano research materials.

Unquestionably, the major attempt at a comprehensive study of the Chicano to date—although it lacks an adequate historical perspective—is Leo Grebler *et al., The Mexican-American People: The Nation's Second Largest Minority,* which was financed by the Ford Foundation and produced by the Mexican-American Studies Project at the University of California, Los Angeles. Before this work appeared in 1970, only Carey McWilliams's *North from Mexico*, published in 1949, provided a reasonably comprehensive account of the Chicano experience. During the years between the publication of *North from Mexico* and *The Mexican-American People*, little serious historical research found its way into print until the latter 1960s when the rise of Chicano militancy was accompanied by the appearance of such works as Ernesto Galarza's *Merchants of Labor: The Mexican Bracero Story* (San Jose, 1964) and Leonard Pitt's *Decline of the Californios: A Social History of the Spanish-Speaking Californians, 1846–1890* (Berkeley and Los Angeles, 1966).

There seems to be a clear correlation between the paucity of publications on Chicano history before the 1960s and the limited number of scholars dedicated to this area of study. Until recently, foundations and publishers were not interested in identifying and supporting qualified scholars who were doing research on Mexican American topics. Indeed, not until Chicano student activists began demanding curriculum changes did a significant number of historians begin to write research proposals and to attract the attention of publishers. For the most part, scholars entering the field have been young, and many of them have been burdened with the responsibility of developing Chicano studies programs in their colleges and universities. The results of their research are only now beginning to appear, and we can expect the output to increase as the large number of Chicano scholars now in graduate schools complete their dissertations. Thus, the nine valuable articles that constitute this book are merely a harbinger of much more that is to come.

In the first essay, "Mexican-American History: An Assessment," Arthur F. Corwin, who has long been involved in the study of Chicano history and historiography, provides readers with the first detailed overview of the development and current status of the art. On a canvas of vast size, he paints a picture which emphasizes the importance of Carey McWilliams and delineates the ways in which scholars are moving away from older simplistic explanations toward deeper, more complex interpretations. Rodolfo Acuña, a leading Chicano historian, challenges some of Corwin's assessments and generalizations, especially his division of historians of the Chicano experience into "La Raza" and "establishment" schools.

Arguing for historical (as well as ethnic) pluralism in the writing of Chicano history, Acuña accuses Corwin of being insensitive and contradictory in many of his appraisals. Taken together, the essays by Corwin and Acuña illustrate the sometimes controversial and polemical environment in which Chicano history is being written today.

In "Once a Well-Kept Secret," Carey McWilliams, editor of the *The Nation* and "Anglo" foster father of Chicano historical studies, describes the genesis of his epochal *North from Mexico*. Though the book met with considerable apathy when it appeared in 1949, it soon elevated him in the eyes of many people to spokesman for minority peoples, especially the Chicano. McWilliams categorically rejects such a role and argues cogently that minorities must develop their own spokesmen. A truly democratic society will be achieved, he concludes, only when Mexican Americans and all minorities are able to participate fully in the economic, cultural, and political mainstream of American life.

Carlos Eduardo Castañeda is without question one of the outstanding Mexican American scholars of the past century. In his study of Castañeda's formative years, Félix D. Almaráz, Jr., himself an important contemporary Mexican American historian, describes Castañeda's incredible drive to overcome the serious financial and personal problems that threatened to block his attempt to become a university teacher of history. Almaráz details Castañeda's youthful desire to achieve academic distinction, his devotion to family, and his relationship with Professor Eugene C. Barker, whose faith in the young man encouraged him to persevere and, finally, to graduate from the University of Texas in 1921. For the next half dozen years, Castañeda continued to face adversity, but he also began to make his mark as a scholar and to attract the attention of his alma mater. In 1927 the University of Texas invited him to return, first as librarian of the Latin American collection and later as a faculty member.

In "Patrón Leadership at the Crossroads: Southern Colorado in the Late Nineteenth Century," William B. Taylor and Elliott West explore one of the many important and heretofore neglected aspects of Chicano history. Theirs is a fascinating account of patrón society as it functioned under the influence of an Anglo as well as a Mexican American. This carefully researched essay describes the changes that occurred in southern Colorado between the early 1860s and the turn of the century as social relationships responded to new economic conditions and the influx of new settlers.

"Working on El Traque: The Pacific Electric Strike of 1903," by California historian Charles Wollenberg, touches upon another largely unexplored area of Chicano history—the Mexican and Chicano railroad worker—and describes in some detail an important incident that took place in Los Angeles at the beginning of this century. Wollenberg characterizes early Mexican railroad workers as forerunners of the great twentieth-century migration and as initiators of more than seventy years of class and ethnic struggle.

A careful study of repatriation and deportation in Los Angeles is the subject of Abraham Hoffman's "Stimulus to Repatriation: The 1931 Federal Deportation Drive and the Los Angeles Mexican Community." Hoffman graphically describes how local authorities devised a scare campaign calculated to frighten illegal Mexican immigrants in the Los Angeles area into voluntary repatriation. He shows us that, despite assurances to the contrary and despite the Mexican government's concern, Mexican aliens were singled out for repatriation in an effort to reduce unemployment in the Los Angeles area. The deportation drive, Hoffman concludes, succeeded in encouraging self-repatriation, but did not appreciably reduce Los Angeles's unemployment. In something of a companion piece, "From Discrimination to Repatriation: Mexican Life in Gary, Indiana, During the Great Depression," historians Neil Betten and Raymond A. Mohl describe the sad plight of urban Mexicans in the Midwest. Like their counterparts in Los Angeles, they were urged to leave because they were allegedly unassimilable, took jobs away from U.S. citizens, and caused relief costs to soar.

Finally, in " 'Mexican American' and 'Chicano': Emerging Terms for a People Coming of Age," geographer Richard L. Nostrand discusses in a historical context the perennial question of a self-reference term for members of La Raza. According to Nostrand, the most important factor in determining self-reference terms in the Southwest has been the different historical experiences of Mexican Americans in Arizona, California, Colorado, New Mexico, and Texas. The author points to recent wide acceptance of the terms "Mexican American" and "Chicano" as evidence that La Raza is a "minority coming of age." Those who identify with these terms, he concludes, "accept, even assert (as in the case with 'Chicano'), their Mexican heritage."

Inevitably this collection of essays does not include all aspects of the long and varied history of Chicanos, but it does serve to provide some fresh, perhaps controversial, perspectives on many important topics. As suggested in the opening article, Chicano history is still in its infancy and many areas of research have barely been scratched. Thus, this collection is all the more welcome as a significant contribution to the expanding study of Chicano history.

MATT MEIER

University of Santa Clara

FELICIANO RIVERA

San Jose State University

Mexican-American History: An Assessment

Arthur F. Corwin

The author is a member of the history department in the University of Connecticut and director of the project for the cooperative study of Mexican migration to the U.S., 1900–1970.

GENERAL HISTORIES

The most remarkable fact about Mexican-American history is Carey McWilliams.[1] For a full generation McWilliams was the "sole authority" in this field, a sort of Lone Ranger coming to the aid of a neglected people by writing the first general history of Mexican Americans. As it turned out, his book, *North from Mexico: The Spanish-Speaking People of the United States* (Lippincott, 1949; reprinted by Greenwood Press, 1968), was no pedestrian survey, but, rather, an inspired synthesis of the Mexican-American heritage. Today, depending on one's point of view, this work is considered either a classic of southwestern history, or a classic of social-protest literature, or both. More to the point, this single volume has exercised an extraordinary influence over the emergent profession of Mexican-American studies.

North from Mexico traces and interprets the full sweep of Mexican-American history from Spanish colonial times to World War II with the ultimate purpose of providing the general public with an exposé of social inequality and economic exploitation imposed on Mexican-descent groups by monopolistic landgrabbers

---

[1] A resumé of McWilliams' writings on Mexican Americans and other ethnic groups is given by Joseph P. Navarro, "The Contributions of Carey McWilliams to American Ethnic History," *Journal of Mexican American History*, II (Fall 1971), 1–21.

and agro-capitalists who were, according to McWilliams, the real conquerors of the borderlands. But this work, which utilized most of the then-available sources, is much more than a socialist critique of the Anglo socio-economic establishment, particularly in California, it is also an impressive work of historical interpretation, brilliantly written by a free-lance historian.

In this work McWilliams fathered what might be called the "frontier thesis" of Chicano history: Mexicans since colonial times have migrated north over familiar land with little or no sense of changing frontiers. This thesis overlooks many frontier facts of north Mexico and the borderlands—for instance, the Spanish and Mexican retreat in desert regions before marauding Indians, sparse Spanish-speaking population in north Mexico and the borderlands, the geographical obstacles to Hispano-Mexican expansion pointed out by Walter Prescott Webb in *The Great Plains* (Ginn and Co., 1931), and the seduction, recruitment, and transportation of several million campesinos for work in American mines, railroads, agriculture, industry, and domestic service. But no matter, this thesis is eagerly accepted by those who would have it serve not only a prior ethnic claim to the southwestern frontier, but also as a rationale for transforming "wetback migration" into "natural migration."

Another important and widely-accepted theme found in McWilliams is that Anglo agribusiness virtually enserfed Mexican migrant labor on the very estates that once belonged to Spain and Mexico. Needless to say, ethnic militants have not hesitated to incorporate this interpretation—from a distinguished Anglo himself—into didactic lectures on Anglo exploitation of La Raza. *North from Mexico* is also esteemed for its devastating, delightful, and debunking critique of the "fantasy heritage," that is, the romantic tradition of the old Southwest propagated by Anglo writers, southwestern chambers of commerce, and Hollywood scenarios that dwell fawningly on imaginary Spanish dons and Spanish fiestas but look askance at Mexican settlers and their culture.

Readers in Mexico can also savor McWilliams' version of how Anglo invaders took over the borderlands and exploited innocent natives and incoming migrant recruits in "their own native land" in a Spanish edition that bears a more militant subtitle: *Al Norte de México, el conflicto entre "anglos" e "hispanos"* (Siglo XXI Editores, 1968). Also facilitating the diffusion of McWilliamismo—the closest thing thus far to an orthodox view of Raza history—is a twenty-minute film for all levels of education, *North from Mexico, Exploration and Heritage* (Educational Film Division, Greenwood Press, 1970).

College-level surveys of Mexican-American history were at first taught, *de rigueur*, with McWillliams' book, plus a makeshift reading list that might have included Eric R. Wolf's anthropological history of the Indo-Mexican race, *Sons of the Shaking Earth* (University of Chicago Press, 1959); some selections on the Mexican War; and readings from such ethnic textbooks as *La Raza: Forgotten Americans* (Notre Dame University Press, 1966), edited by sociologist Julian Samora; *Mexican Americans in the United States, a Reader* (Schenkman, 1970), edited by John H. Burma; *The Mexican-American People: The Nation's Second Largest Minority* (Free Press–Macmillan, 1970), a UCLA Mexican-American Study Project directed by Leo Grebler; or *Mexican-Americans in the Southwest* (McNally & Loftin, 1969, 1970), a concise report prepared by Ernesto Galarza, Herman Gallegos, and Julian Samora. These readings were commonly supplemented by some war-on-poverty literature and some oral history straight from the mouths of militant spokesmen, as in *La Raza: The Mexican American* (Harper and Row, 1969), by New-Left writer Stan Steiner; or in Armando B. Rendón's *Chicano Manifesto* (Macmillan, 1971). The use of such mixed materials in history courses usually led to a neglect of historical causality and an overemphasis on the twentieth-century social conditions of Mexican Americans and their struggle for civil rights and political power.

The first college-level texts rushed into print for Mexican-American history have reduced the dependence on McWilliams and have eliminated to some degree the indiscriminate mixing in survey courses of *non sequiturs* from historical, sociological, and political literature. On the other hand, most new texts have not seriously questioned the McWilliams' concept that Mexican-American history is principally a history of unrelieved exploitation. Nor have they overcome the biggest *non sequitur* of all, namely, that the historical heritage of the massive La Raza or Chicano migration that flowed in from twentieth-century Mexico is somehow the direct lineal descendant of the historical experience of Hispanos, Tejanos, and Californios settled in small, isolated, enclaves on the distant rim of the Spanish empire.

The reluctance to distinguish between one heritage and another should not be attributed to McWilliams, but rather to the present doctrinaire nature of ethnic studies. Some ethnic historians and political leaders prefer to minimize distinctions between southwestern Indians, early Hispano-Mexican settlers, and the later La Raza migrations, not merely because to some extent Indo-American peoples were all exploited or dominated by Anglos, but principally —or so it would seem—because cultural or historical identity, real or imagined, with earlier native settlers makes for a more convincing ethnic claim on the Southwest and on national attention, especially under the Treaty of Guadalupe Hidalgo or under the Aztlán mythology of the return of the native Aztecs. In any case, this phenomenon is not exactly new.[2]

The first published syllabus, *A Documentary History of the Mexican Americans* (Praeger, 1970), by professional editors Wayne Moquín and Charles Van Doren, with an introductory blessing by Mexican-American historian Feliciano Rivera of California State University, San Jose, perpetuates the great *non sequitur* in a typically unbalanced format that perhaps can be partly excused by the lack of historical studies on twentieth-century Mexican Americans. In any case, three-fifths of this book of very readable but mostly irrelevant selections—taken from the common stuff of preexisting "Anglo courses" on borderland history—are devoted to the frontier doings of Spanish explorers, adventurers, and missionaries, and Anglo-American penetrators with no firm connection whatever shown between frontier events and personalities and twentieth-century economic developments in the Southwest (not to mention a Mexican Revolution) that gave rise to the Raza labor proletariat. After pointing out how the Spanish-speaking natives were victimized by a false treaty and land fraud, a leap is then made, a la McWilliams, to the exploitation of Mexican laborers and their marginal condition in national society. Such slants, repeatedly labored in the introductory paragraphs, but without adequate or objective documentation, would give the erroneous impression that twentieth-century social conditions of "cheap alien labor" recruited from Mexico (and the Philippines, the Orient, and the depressed south-

---

2 Some examples that come readily to mind are the search for a more ancient and respectable genealogy by the emergent Aztec and Roman city-states as well as the claims of various European immigrant groups that one of their ancestors discovered America first.

ern states) are somehow the direct, evil result of an unjust frontier conflict over a nearly-empty territory. Of the two or three random selections on Mexican labor, characteristically one of them happens to be McWilliams' oversimplified account of Mexican repatriation during the 1930s. The remainder of the book is more concerned with illustrating present social conditions and political militancy.

The compressed readings (68 in all) in Julian Nava's rather brief, introductory work on the cultural roots of the Chicano, *¡Viva la Raza! Readings on Mexican Americans* (Van Nostrand, 1973), are, overall, more relevant and the introductory remarks more restrained than in the Moquin book. And for the most part, educator-historian Nava strives to maintain historical perspective in his selections which range from El Cid to somewhere near Corky González. Also touched upon are such neglected topics as the character of the Spanish conquest and the reformist aims of the Mexican Revolution, and the reader is sometimes given two views of certain controversies, such as the land question after 1848 and labor exploitation. But as the author approaches the current history of *el movimiento,* the olympian detachment rapidly erodes and we have in the final sections yet another collection of protest literature which serves mostly to push such themes of special interest to "The Cause" as the need for Chicano pride, political activism, and (*Porqué no?*) biculturalism in place of a destructive system of Anglo education.

Although *Aztlan: An Anthology of Mexican American Literature* (Knopf Vintage Books, 1972), edited by Luís Valdez with the collaboration of Stan Steiner, makes no claim to being Mexican-American history, it is nevertheless a compilation of snippets from past and present writings that are more historical than literary in nature. To the neophyte this selection, which is now being used in some history courses, may seem to be a *pot pourri* of remotely related events, periods, peoples, and symbols from Aztecs and Mayas through the Spanish borderlands down to the present militant demands for colonial liberation. The one unifying theme of this anthology is the same romantic myth of indigenous nationalism that has animated so much of the literary symbolism and didactic murals of revolutionary Mexico. The Chicano liberation movement, like the *indigenista* movement in Mexico, is umbilically tied to Aztlán, its defeat, its long suffering under colonialism, and its resurrection

—with a special Raza twist—not in Mexico, but in the original homeland of the Aztecs, namely, the Southwest under the new "Plan de Aztlán."[3]

The Mexican-Americans: An Awakening Minority (Glencoe Press, 1970), edited by historian Manuel Servín of Arizona State University, is an example of a more specialized syllabus. This interesting and informative selection of new and old writings, by a mixed group of writers, including McWilliams and Servín himself, traces the emergence of the mestizo race to colonial times but then quickly shifts to the twentieth-century struggle for social advancements against civil disabilities, race prejudice, Texas Rangers, and economic exploitation. This syllabus makes no attempt to explain the persistence of trans-border migration and its possible relation to persistent social problems.

As for narrative textbooks, Ruth S. Lamb's *Mexican Americans: Sons of the Southwest* (Claremont, Calif., Ocelot Press, 1970) earnestly seeks to integrate the Mexican-American past into the Indian and Spanish heritage of Mexico and the Anglo history of the Southwest. This well-written account certainly has more unity than the typical Mexican-American anthology, and there is a proper historical appreciation for "The Great Migration" from twentieth-century Mexico, but it is a survey after all, manifesting no original research, leaning on McWilliams' interpretations of borderlands history, and committing the same venial sin of devoting most of its attention to remote historical heritages that have scant relation to "The Great Migration" of campesinos into the margins of an advanced corporate society. However, in its final pages, this work provides one of the better current-history surveys of the civil-rights march since World War II.

Chicanos, a History of Mexican Americans (Hill and Wang, 1972), by Matt S. Meier of the University of Santa Clara, together with Feliciano Rivera, covers in more detail the Indian, colonial,

---

3 This plan is paraphrased by Valdez in the introduction: "No Statue of Liberty ever greeted our arrival in this country. . . . The United States came to us. We have been in America a long time. Somewhere in the twelfth century our Aztec ancestors left their homeland of Aztlán, and migrated south to Anahuac, 'the place by the waters,' where they built the great city of México-Tenochtitlán. Aztlán was left far behind, somewhere 'in the north,' but it was never forgotten.

"Aztlán is now the name of our Mestizo nation, existing to the north of Mexico, within the borders of the United States. Chicano poets sing of it, and their *flor y canto* points toward new yet very ancient gods. . . ."

and Mexican heritages, the violent Anglo-Mexican confrontation in the borderlands, the Spanish-speaking under American occupation, modern Mexican migration, the revolutionary background, the role of Mexican labor, including braceros and wetbacks, the antecedents of political activism, and present-day militant movements. In the nature of things, this is another wide-ranging account that, again, makes relatively little distinction between the Hispano-Mexican heritage of the old southwestern frontier and the great Raza exodus that seems to have overwhelmed most of it. The authors regard the Chicano heritage as an inextricable blend of historical forces and peoples, namely, the traumatic frontier experience of early Hispano-Mexicans, and the later migratory waves from Mexico which served as cultural reinforcements. Essentially, this interpretation follows the grand design originally laid out by McWilliams, but, in other ways, Meier and Rivera update McWilliams and go beyond his work, especially in their expanded accounts of Mexican labor and political history. In sum, *Chicanos* is the most scholarly and the most thorough of the new ethnic histories thus far.

The theme of *Occupied America: The Chicano's Struggle toward Liberation* (Canfield Press, 1972), by Rodolfo Acuña, California State University, Northridge, is taken from third-world ideology which predicates that underdeveloped peoples are victims of economic imperialism. Lately, a variation on this theme, called "internal colonialism," has been popularized by political activists of many shades. Internal colonialism serves not only to explain the marginality of certain ethnic groups and the mechanism of exploitation, but it also serves to rationalize cultural separatism. The author adds to this a corollary from the economic thought of nationalist Mexico, to wit: Mexico since the days of the dictator Porfirio Díaz (1876–1910) has been an economic colony of the United States, and Anglo-American economic power has forced or pulled defenseless Mexican laborers over the border into the orbit of internal colonialism where they could be used or deported at will.

As Acuña tells it, colonial oppression and deceit began with the taking of Texas and have continued almost uninterrupted down to the present-day police and immigration-enforcement activities in the barrios. In reality, this work is a variation of the "unrelieved exploitation" theme first artfully presented in *North from Mexico*, but, since it lacks restraint, *Occupied America* is more like *McWil-*

liamismo carried from the sublime to the ridiculous. This is regretable, for in some ways Acuña has produced a major work of Chicano scholarship that breaks new ground on such subjects as border conflict, Mexican labor migration, mutual-aid societies, and militant groups, and it is heavily footnoted throughout. But the narrative is spotted with gross exaggerations and a morbid line of quotes taken out of historical context. A possible virtue of this book is that, like Stan Steiner's *La Raza,* it never leaves the reader in doubt as to the Brown Beret's view of southwestern history.

A vivid, non-footnoted, semi-popular account that seeks to cover simultaneously the heritage of all Hispanic peoples in the United States from Ponce de León through César Chávez is Harold J. Alford's *The Proud Peoples: The Heritage and Culture of Spanish-Speaking Peoples in the United States* (David McKay Co., 1972). Unfortunately, this work is too often interrupted by far-fetched references to Puerto Ricans in New York, Cubans in Florida, and Hispanos in landlocked New Mexico. Nevertheless, this synoptic attempt does capture the spirit of the Mexican-American subculture and provides an unusually penetrating account of Mexican migrant labor.

The first Mexican-American history to concentrate exclusively on the era preceding mass migration from Mexico is David Weber's *Foreigners in Their Native Land: Historical Roots of the Mexican American* (University of New Mexico Press, 1973). Well-organized essays and original reading selections cover the period from the first settlements to approximately 1910, but the main points of emphasis are territorial and cultural conflict, the disputed Treaty of Guadalupe Hidalgo, and the civil-rights theme of "strangers in their own land."

We cannot here consider all the survey accounts of the Mexican Americans that have been published by academic and non-academic writers. Nor have we space to consider histories of "ethnic pride" written for pre-college instruction or to list all the promised studies on Mexican Americans.

As for the place of Mexican Americans in national histories, a comparison would show that some standard accounts of the United States have been revised to include more materials on the Negro, but these same histories still tend to say relatively little about the Southwest under Spain and Mexico and virtually nothing about the role of Mexican immigrant labor in southwestern development. Thus far, one of the few regional histories that gives anywhere near adequate representation to the Spanish-speaking in borderland development is Lynn I. Perrigo's *Texas and Our Spanish Southwest* (Banks, Upshaw Co., 1960; slightly revised, updated, and reprinted by Holt, Rinehart and Winston, 1971). On the other hand, a number of state histories of California, Texas, and New Mexico—for example, Erna Fergusson's outstanding *New Mexico: A Pageant of Three Peoples* (2nd ed., Knopf, 1964)—have for years pointed with pride to the Spanish colonial heritage. However, they too have little to say about twentieth-century Mexican Americans. In its revised form, John W. Caughey's *California: A Remarkable State's Life History* (3rd ed., Prentice-Hall, 1970) goes beyond the usual account of California under Spain and Mexico to incorporate observations on contemporary Mexican labor and social conditions up to the celebrated *Huelga* movement. This example seems to point the way to future modifications in national, regional, and state histories.[4]

Again, Mexican-American history has nothing comparable at this time to the annotated compilations and reference works available for Negro history, which, after all, has been institutionalized in black colleges and in the *Journal of Negro History* for more than fifty years. It is true that dozens of Mexican-American or Chicano bibliographical surveys have been rapidly assembled in the past few years by librarians, ethnic study groups, and lecturers in southwestern universities and cities to meet pressing demands for instruc-

---

[4] An example of a national history that has added materials on Mexican Americans is *Many Pasts: Readings in American Social History* (2 vols., Prentice-Hall, 1972), by Herbert Gutman and Gregory S. Kealey. Volume II of this textbook contains historian John Womack's chapter on "Who are the Chicanos?" Standard regional histories, such as W. Eugene Hollon's *The Southwest: Old and New* (Alfred A. Knopf, 1961; University of Nebraska Press, 1968), give only a passing nod to Mexicans in the modern Southwest, although Odie B. Faulk's *Land of Many Frontiers* (Oxford University Press, 1968) and Gerald D. Nash's more recent *The American West in the Twentieth Century: A Short History of an Urban Oasis* (Prentice-Hall, 1973) give somewhat more representation. Examples of state histories that have worked in fuller references to contemporary Mexican Americans are Warren A. Beck and David A. Williams, *California: A History of the Golden State* (Doubleday, 1972); Andrew F. Rolle, *California: A History* (Rev. ed., Crowell, 1969); and Walton Bean, *California: An Interpretive History* (2nd ed., McGraw-Hill, 1972). For the place of Mexican Americans in other general works, see Abraham Hoffman, "Where are the Mexican Americans? A Textbook Omission Overdue for Revision," *History Teacher*, VI (1972), 143–150.

tional materials, but with some exceptions these reading lists are repetitious, eclectic, uncritical, and non-annotated.[5]

In the meantime, some historians, dissatisfied with general compilations "of all that is at hand on Mexicans in the United States, irrelevant or not," have begun to piece together specialized bibliographical tools for the teaching of Mexican-American history. Thus far, the most impressive work is a non-annotated compilation by Matt S. Meier, assisted by Feliciano Rivera, *A Selective Bibliography for the Study of Mexican American History* (Spartan Book Store, San Jose, California State University, 1971; reprinted in amplified form by R and E Associates of San Francisco, 1972).

An annotated bibliography devoted exclusively to Mexican-American history has not yet been published, although this purpose is partly served by certain annotated surveys of the leading works on Mexican Americans by social scientists, historians, and others. These include *The Mexican American, A Selected and Annotated Bibliography,* edited and revised by Luis G. Nogales (Stanford University Press, 1971), which presents, all in all, an objective appraisal; and Ernie Barrios and others, *Bibliografía de Aztlán: An Annotated Chicano Bibliography* (California State University, San Diego, Centro de Estudios Chicanos, 1971), an extensive compilation by students and instructors that is intended to be a full Chicano critique of the significant literature on Mexican Americans.

General listings of useful bibliographies have appeared in Chicano publications. There is, for example, Joseph A. Clark y Moreno's "Bibliography of Bibliographies Relating to Mexican American Studies," *El Grito,* III (Summer, 1970), 25–31, which includes eighty-eight non-annotated items in English. Ron Padilla's "Apuntes para la documentación de la cultura chicano," *El Grito,* V (Winter, 1971–1972), 3–79, is a partly-annotated monograph, published in English, that contains, taken together with Clark y Moreno's work, perhaps the most complete list to date of the many

---

[5] Some of the more useful of many recent ethnic compilations are: *A Guide to Materials Relating to Persons of Mexican Heritage in the United States,* compiled by the Inter-Agency Committee on Mexican American Affairs (Washington, D.C., 1969), a non-annotated but broad survey especially designed for educators; Ralph Guzmán, *Revised Bibliography* (Advance Report 3, Mexican American Study Project, Graduate School of Business Research, University of California, Los Angeles, 1967), a comprehensive but non-annotated work reprinted in Grebler, *et al., The Mexican-American People;* and Heminio Ríos and Lupe Castillo, "Toward a True Chicano Bibliography—Mexican American Newspapers, 1848–1942," *El Grito,* III (Summer 1970), 17–24.

bibliographies that have proliferated in response to the sudden demand for materials on Mexican Americans. In addition, Padilla offers a near-exhaustive listing of earlier bibliographical works, some of which, in a brief, salty, introductory essay, are classified as relevant, that is, Raza-oriented (*Nihil obstat*), or irrelevant, that is, Anglo-oriented (*Gabacho*).

Published guides for Mexican-American history do not yet go beyond some simplistic handbooks to meet the uncertainties of teachers suddenly charged with inculcating ethnic studies. Examples would be Carey McWilliams' *The Mexicans in America: A Student's Guide to Localized History* (Teacher's College Press, Columbia University, 1968) and ethnic-anthropologist Jack D. Forbes' *Mexican-Americans: A Handbook for Educators* (Berkeley, Far West Laboratory for Educational Research and Development, 1967). On the other hand, some Chicano publications are intended to be partial guides for university students. One example is the annotated *Bibliografía de Aztlán,* by Ernie Barrios and others. Another instance is the extensive article by Juan Gómez-Quiñones, entitled "Toward a Perspective on Chicano History," *Aztlán,* II (Fall 1971), 1–49. This latter study is not only an impressive attempt to conceptualize, periodize, and evaluate the state of La Raza history, but it is also a critical commentary on many primary and secondary sources for the period 1600 to the present.

TOPICAL STUDIES AND PRESENT RESEARCH NEEDS

What has been done in historical writing relevant to Mexican Americans prior to, or independent of, the ethnic movement, and what needs to be done can perhaps best be appreciated through a topical analysis of published and unpublished literature. At the same time we will point out some research needs or opportunities.

The Indian heritage of the Southwest has thus far been of marginal importance to Mexican-American studies. The same can be said of Mayas, Tarascans, Yaquis, and hundreds of Mexican Indian groups which mixed with Spaniards to form the mestizo race. Here it is evident that Mexican nationalism and its glorification of Aztec civilization were carried over the border by La Raza. Furthermore, this centering on the "highest Indian culture" is reinforced by the search for ethnic pride and identity. In any case, Aztec symbolism, much as it is in Mexico, is stamped all over Chicano literature.

Aztec imagery, therefore, is of fundamental importance to La

Raza ideology and indoctrination. Yet in a wider sense, all forms of
Indian survivals from Mexico are relevant to Chicano studies. Here
we cannot list the vast literature on the subject of mythological and
cultural survivals. We can only suggest several interpretive studies
of the Aztecs by writers like Miguel León-Portilla and Benjamin
Keen, and studies of Indo-Spanish syncretism by writers like Anita
Brenner and Francisco de la Maza. Such works are currently of
special interest to students of the Indo-Mexican heritage.[6]

The Spanish Southwest immediately raises questions about the
relevancy of the distinguished histories by Hubert Howe Bancroft,
Herbert Eugene Bolton, Eugene Barker, Charles Hackett, George
Hammond, H. I. Priestly, Charles Chapman, John Caughey, Robert
Cleland, W. W. Robinson, Maynard Geiger, Peter M. Dunne, and
many others. This borderlands literature, conveniently summarized
in John F. Bannon, *The Spanish Borderlands Frontier, 1513–1812*
(Holt, Rinehart and Winston, 1970), 257–287, is rejected, *a priori*,
by many students of ethnic history because it is regarded as Anglo
history, or because such history says too much about the deeds of
Spanish conquerors and missionaries and not enough about the
social history of submerged Indian and mestizo groups. (See, for example, the comments in Barrios and others, *Bibliografía de Aztlán*).
On the other hand, what serious scholar in search of the roots of the
mestizo or Mexican race could ignore salient studies that either
illuminate the frontier as a social process or that document the formative influences in southwestern religion, law, and agriculture
that today constitute the institutional legacy of Hispano-Mexican
pioneers. One has in mind here the creative works of such borderland historians as Herbert E. Bolton, Walter Prescott Webb, and
Paul Horgan, and of such cultural anthropologists as Eric Wolf,

---

[6] See, for example, León-Portilla, *Aztec Thought and Culture: A Study of the
Ancient Nahuatl Mind* (University of Oklahoma, 1963), and his *Broken Spears* (Bea-
con Press, 1969), an Aztec view of the conquest as preserved by Spanish chroniclers;
Keen, *The Aztec Image* (Rutgers University Press, 1971), a monumental intellectual
history of the Aztecs in New World and European literature; Brenner, *Idols behind
Altars* (Harpers, 1929), and De la Maza, *El guadalupanismo mexicano* (México, D. F.,
Porrua y Obregón, 1953). The latter two works are concerned with Indo-Spanish
religious survivals. The revolutionary vision of a new nationalism emerging from the
fusion of Indian, Hispanic, and other ethnic elements is exemplified in such writings
as *La raza cósmica* (México, 1922), by José Vasconcelos; and *Forjando patria: Pro
nacionalismo* (México, 1916), by Manuel Gamio.

Edward Spicer, and Jack Forbes.[7] There are also notable histories, interpretations, and documentary collections by François Chevalier, L. B. Simpson, Silvio Zavala, Benjamin Keen, Charles Gibson, Lewis Hanke, George Foster, and others that illustrate the Spanish conquest and the Indo-Hispano origins of peonage labor, as well as the hacienda system that pervaded the utmost reaches of New Spain.[8]

Diverse perspectives in time and place on the survival in the borderlands of distinct ethnic groups, including Indians, Mexicans, Mormons, and others are discussed in *Plural Society in the Southwest* (Interbook Inc., 1972). This symposium containing contributions by noted anthropologists and historians like Edward Spicer, Miguel León-Portilla, John H. Parry, and Ernesto Galarza also suggests topics for historical research.

The Southwest under Mexico, 1821–1848, is, from the viewpoint of Mexican-American history, one of the least studied periods. In the past, both Mexican and American historians have tended to see this era merely as one of institutional decay and military retreat before marauding tribes and Anglo infiltrators, or as a prologue to the territorial cession of 1848. Although much travel lore and many

---

[7] Some important examples would be Herbert E. Bolton's "The Mission as a Frontier Institution," *American Historical Review*, XXIII (1917), 42–61, which stands as an original thesis on the institutional technique of Spanish expansion into primitive regions; Walter Prescott Webb's unique corollary to the Turner thesis, *The Great Plains* (1931), which emphasizes physical and Indian obstacles to Spanish and Mexican settlement, and the later impact of technology in the decisive conquest and development of this geographical barrier; and Paul Horgan's dramatic work, *Great River: The Rio Grande in North American History* (2 vols., Holt, Rinehart and Winston, 1954), especially volume one entitled "Indians and Spain." Important works on the colonial process of race mixture and the formation of the Mexican people would include C. W. Marshall's "The Birth of the Mestizo in New Spain," *Hispanic American Historical Review*, XIX (1939), 161–184; Magnus Moërner's *Race Mixture in the History of Latin American* (Little, Brown, 1967); and Richard Konetzke, ed. *Colección de documentos para la historia social de Hispanoamerica, 1493–1810* (3 vols., Madrid, 1962); and relevant works by such cultural anthropologists as Wolf, *Sons of the Shaking Earth*, a stimulating interpretation of the social and economic evolution of colonial Mexico; Edward H. Spicer, *Cycles of Conquest: The Impact of Spain, Mexico, and the United States on the Indians of the Southwest, 1533–1960* (University of Arizona Press, 1962), a suggestive comparison of colonial policies; and Jack D. Forbes, *Apache, Navajo, and Spaniard* (University of Oklahoma Press, 1960), a study of frontier transculturation.

[8] These and many other relevant works can be found in annotated form in Charles C. Griffin, ed., *Latin America, A Guide to the Historical Literature* (University of Texas Press, 1971); see also George M. Foster, *Culture of Conquest: America's Spanish Heritage* (Wenner-Gren Foundation, 1960).

histories of California, New Mexico, and Texas have touched on the late mission period, the dons of California, the ricos of New Mexico, and Mexican and Anglo land speculators, there is no major history of this period. This seems due in part to the scarcity of written records and to the small Spanish-speaking population that numbered no more than 80,000 in 1848, with about two-thirds of this number concentrated in a northern New Mexico enclave. Mexico's northern territories, indeed, posed a formidable problem in colonization and mixing of races, and it is precisely this perspective that prevails in the important monographs on this period by such historians as C. Alan Hutchinson, Eugene C. Barker, Vito Alessio Robles, and Samuel H. Lowrie.[9]

Naturally, the causes of the war with Mexico have been a subject of consuming interest to many teachers of Mexican-American studies. Earlier works concerned with the unfolding of the conflict by Justin Smith, E. C. Barker, and George L. Rives have usually been dismissed as history written for the Anglo establishment. On the other hand, those histories that give both sides of the dispute, or the Mexican account of it, are more in line with the present revisionist objectives of ethnic studies. Among such works are Ramón Ruiz, ed., *The Mexican War—Was It Manifest Destiny?* (Holt, Rinehart and Winston, 1963); Glenn W. Price, *Origins of the War with Mexico: The Polk-Stockton Intrigue* (University of Texas Press, 1967); Otis A. Singletary, *The Mexican War* (University of Chicago Press, 1960); *The Mexican Side of the Texan Revolution by the Chief Mexican Participants* . . . (Dallas, 1928), edited by the late Carlos Castañeda, a distinguished Latin Americanist; and *Recuerdos de la invasión norteamericana, 1841–1848, por un joven de entonces* (México, 1883; reprinted by Editorial Porrua, 3 vols.,

---

[9] C. Alan Hutchinson, *Frontier Settlement in Mexican California: The Hijar-Padrés Colony and Its Origins, 1789–1835* (Yale University Press, 1969) is a factual account of Mexican efforts to colonize and hold Alta California; Eugene C. Barker, *The Life of Stephen F. Austin, Founder of Texas, 1793–1836: A Chapter in the Westward Movement of the American People* (Dallas, 1925; reprinted by the University of Texas Press, 1971), is a definitive study of Austin's colony and the empresario's relations with successive Mexican governments; Vito Alessio Robles, *Coahuila y Texas, desde la consumación de la independencia hasta el tratado de paz de Guadalupe Hildalgo* (2 vols., México, 1946), is an account of frontier problems, land-grant policies, and the Anglo colonization threat; and Samuel H. Lowrie, *Culture Conflict in Texas, 1821–1835* (New York, 1932), is similar in emphasis to the work by Vito Alessio Robles. See also Lynn R. Bailey, *Indian Slave Trade in the Southwest* (Westernlore Press, 1966), a survey of a neglected facet of Indian-Mexican relations in the disputed territories.

1947), a contemporary Mexican account by José María Roa Barcena. Although the war with Mexico is clearly the most studied topic of this period, there is now an obvious need for a major interpretive critique that would integrate conflicting interpretations and source materials. A beginning has been made by Seymour V. Connor and Odie B. Faulk in a brief revisionist account of the causes of the war. But the principal contribution of their *North America Divided: The Mexican War* (Oxford University Press, 1971) is an extensive bibliographical compilation of North American and Mexican sources that the authors regard as an important preliminary step to future revisionist studies.

American occupation and development of the borderlands from about 1848 to 1910—that is, the history of the Spanish-speaking under the domination of Anglo-American economic, social, and political institutions—are, according to some ethnic scholars, the proper starting points of La Raza history.[10] The disposal of Spanish and Mexican land grants is, of course, a heated subject, especially since visionary Reies Tijerina, beginning in 1965, dramatized the land-claims question in New Mexico with almost biblical appeals to the sacred guarantees of the Treaty of Guadalupe Hidalgo. Militants hold that the Spanish-speaking (who, whether *ricos* or *peones,* were apparently all here in 1848) were stripped of their land and their culture in violation of the articles of the 1848 treaty and forced from Arcadia into the landless peasantry, or into migrant work, or into the Anglo-American melting pot. Writers like McWilliams, Stan Steiner, Clark S. Knowlton, and Richard Gardner, for example, have tended to support this interpretation.[11]

The treaty itself has been reprinted with an historical introduction and explanatory notes by George P. Hammond, *The Treaty of Guadalupe Hidalgo, 1848* (University of California Press, 1949), and recently at least two other editions have appeared.[12] But thus

---

10 Anglo-American literature on occupation and development of the Southwest is described by Ray A. Billington in an historiographical essay appended to his *The Far Western Frontier, 1830–1860* (Harper and Row, 1956), 293–311.

11 Knowlton has written several articles on land loss in New Mexico and its socio-economic implications. See, for example, "Land Grant Problems Among the State's Spanish Speaking," *New Mexico Business*, XX (1967), 1–13. Gardner's ¡*Grito! Reies Tijerina and the New Mexico Land Grant War of 1967* (Bobbs-Merrill, 1970) is perhaps the most carefully researched of recent journalistic accounts of this protest movement.

12 *Guadalupe Hidalgo Treaty of Peace, 1848, and the Gadsen Treaty with Mexico,*

far this disputed document has not been the subject of a major analytical monograph in legal history or international law directed
specifically toward the question of ethnic claims.

There is no general history of southwestern land grants, plainly
a most difficult challenge, for land history differs considerably in
California, Texas, and New Mexico. On the other hand, there are
numerous state and regional histories that cover political machina-
tions and social and economic facets of land-grant turnovers.[13]

Two outstanding studies have shown what can be done with the
"lost generation" of the occupation period. In *The Decline of the
Californios: A Social History of Spanish-Speaking Californians,
1848–1890* (University of California Press, 1966), Leonard Pitt
carefully traced the relation between land loss and disintegration
or absorption through inter-marriage of leading Californio families;
and Cecil Robinson, in his *With the Ears of Strangers: The Mexican in American Literature* (University of Arizona Press, 1969),
uncovered the origins of many images and stereotypes of Mexicans
in Anglo-American literature of the occupation period—images and
stereotypes that have since been perpetuated in travel accounts, romantic novels, and Hollywood horse operas. Also, a study of a leading California statesman, *Vallejo: Son of California* (Portland, Biu-
fords and Mort, 1944), by Myrtle M. McKittrick,[14] suggests that if
papers are available biographies could be written about prominent
Tejano, Californio, or Hispano families of this period.

Celebrated collections of folklore by J. Frank Dobie, Charles F.
Lummis, Arthur L. Campa, Jovita González, and others suggest the

1853 (Truchas, New Mex., Tate Gallery, 1968); and *El Tratado de Guadalupe Hidalgo,
1848: Treaty of Guadalupe Hidalgo, 1848—A Facsimile Reproduction of the Mexican
Instrument of Ratification and Related Documents* (Sacramento, California State
Department of Education, 1968).

13 Some examples are Howard R. Lamar, *Far Southwest, 1846–1912: A Territorial
History* (Yale University Press, 1966), which considers land-grant questions in New
Mexico, Colorado, and Arizona; Victor Westphall, *Public Domain in New Mexico,
1891–1954* (University of New Mexico Press, 1966); William W. Robinson, *Land in
California: The Story of Mission Lands, Ranchos, Squatters, Mining Claims, Railroad
Grants, Land Scrip and Homesteads* (University of California Press, 1948); Paul W.
Gates, "Adjudication of Spanish-Mexican Land Claims in California," *Huntington
Library Quarterly*, XXI (1958), 213–236; and Thomas L. Miller, *The Public Lands of
Texas* (University of Oklahoma Press, 1971). See also a special issue on land and water
in New Mexico by Richard E. Greenleaf, Myra E. Jenkins, Marc Simmons, Morris
Taylor, and others in the *New Mexico Historical Review*, XLVII (April 1972), 85–201.
All the above works suggest further sources.

14 There is *A Guide to the Mariano Guadalupe Vallejo Documentos para la Historia de California, 1780–1875* (University of California Press, 1953), by Doris M.
Wright. The Vallejo papers are housed in the Bancroft Library.

richness of Mexican folklore in the occupation period.[15] The folk heroes who resisted the "Anglo Conquest" presently hold most appeal for the Raza school of Mexican-American studies. Witness, for example, the popularity of folklorist Américo Paredes' study of a Mexican border ballad that celebrates the triumph of a native Tejano over a Texas Ranger, hated symbol of Anglo domination along the Rio Grande. *With His Pistol in His Hand—A Border Ballad and Its Hero* (University of Texas Press, 1958) literally points the way toward a series of future monographs on the heroes of the resistance. Consider for a moment the ethnic-history potential of Padre José Antonio Martínez, the suspected instigator of the Taos rebellion against the newly-established territorial government of New Mexico; or Joaquín Murieta (Californio? Sonoran?) in the role of Chicano defender of the Spanish-speaking minority overrun by greedy gold rushers;[16] or Mexican-border hero Juan Nepomuceno Cortina, the "Red-bearded Raider," who terrorized Brownsville, Texas, in the 1850s and humiliated a detachment of pursuing Texas *Rinches.*[17]

Just how and under what conditions several million Mexicans have migrated to the United States in the twentieth century is—strange to say—only now beginning to attract the serious attention of professional historians, even though the implications of modern Mexican migration would seem to be enormous. For one thing, La Raza consciousness, deeply-rooted in the "Conquest Culture" of Mexico, to use George Foster's phrase, has, except in insulated areas like the upper Rio Grande valley, literally overwhelmed and absorbed the small enclaves of Spanish-speaking natives of the old Southwest. For another, perennial migration seems to be not only one logical starting point of Chicano history, but a principal dy-

---

15 Much of this folklore is annotated by Dobie in *Guide to Life and Literature of the Southwest* (Rev. ed., Southern Methodist University Press, 1958); and Mabel Major and T. M. Pearce, *Southwest Heritage: A Literary History with Bibliography* (3rd ed., University of New Mexico Press, 1972).

16 The literature on folk heroes is analyzed by E. K. Francis, "Padre Martínez: A New Mexican Myth," *New Mexico Historical Review,* XXXI (1956), 265–289; and Joseph H. Jackson, "The Creation of Joaquín Murieta," *Pacific Spectator,* II (1948), 176–180. See also Pedro Castillo and Albert Camarillo, eds., *Furia y Muerte: Los Bandidos Chicanos* (Aztlán Publications, Monograph No. 4, Chicano Studies Center, University of California, Los Angeles, 1973).

17 Three Anglo-American historians who have appraised Cortina's career are Walter Prescott Webb, *The Texas Rangers: A Century of Frontier Defense* (Houghton Mifflin, 1935; reprinted by University of Texas Press, 1965); Clarence C. Clenenden, *Blood on the Border: The United States Army and Mexican Irregulars* (Macmillan, 1969); and Charles Goldfinch, *Juan N. Cortina, 1824–1892: A Reappraisal* (Brownsville: Bishop's Print Shop, 1950).

namic of the unique barrio subculture established in the twentieth-century Southwest.

The fact that general histories of immigration say much about transatlantic migration and formative influences from Europe but little or nothing about the great flow over the Mexican border should perhaps not raise an eyebrow. For trans-border migration from Mexico (or Quebec) came through the "back door," so to speak, much of it invisible or uncounted, and for the most part it played, until World War II and the farm-labor movement, a rather inconspicuous role as a rural and industrial labor proletariat that flowed back and forth over the border, or across the Midwest and Southwest not unlike the Italian golondrinas who worked in Argentine agriculture.

And yet, beginning with Victor L. Clark's report of 1908, certain social scientists were quick to sense the socio-economic importance of mass labor-migration from Mexico. Even more indispensable for an historical understanding of the phenomenon are the field studies published by Paul S. Taylor (1928–1934) and Manuel Gamio (1930–1931).[18] Social scientists like Norman D. Humphrey and

18 Victor S. Clark, an economist, first called attention to the rapid spread of Mexican peon labor in the border states and beyond in "Mexican Labor in the United States," U.S. Bureau of Labor *Bulletin No. 78* (Sept. 1908), 466–522. Max S. Handman, a sociologist with the University of Texas, classified emigrants according to social groups and explained the causes of wage-labor emigration in two pioneering articles: "The Mexican Immigrant in Texas," *Southwestern Political and Social Science Quarterly*, VIII (1926), 33–41; and "Economic Reasons for the Coming of the Mexican Immigrant," *American Journal of Sociology*, XXXV (1930), 601–605.

By far the most significant of the early social-science studies is the multi-volumed series by economist Paul S. Taylor of the University of California, Berkeley. His work, *Mexican Labor in the United States*, was published in ten parts between 1928 and 1934 by the University of California Press. Based largely on field studies, this series constitutes an invaluable storehouse of first-hand information on the first generation of Mexican migrant labor in California, Texas, Colorado, Pennsylvania, and Illinois. Another significant work by Taylor, *A Mexican-American Frontier, Nueces County, Texas* (University of North Carolina Press, 1934), traced the origins of Mexican labor-use and race relations in south Texas far back into the nineteenth century. Also of fundamental importance are two sourcebooks by the late Manuel Gamio, a distinguished anthropologist from Mexico. The data for his principal study, *Mexican Immigration to the United States: A Study of Human Migration and Adjustment* (University of Chicago, 1930; reprinted by Dover Publications, 1971), were gathered during the years 1926–1927 at the height of the first labor exodus from Mexico. A companion study, *The Mexican Immigrant: His Life Story* (Chicago, 1931; reprinted by Dover Publications, 1971), is a collection of fifty-seven interviews and life stories that illustrate immigrant experiences and feelings about American society.

missionaries like Robert N. McLean also made significant attempts to explain the causes of Mexican emigration.[19]

The fact is that no American historian published anything like an interpretation of Mexican migration until Carey McWilliams' ground-breaking *North from Mexico* (1949). John R. Martínez' doctoral dissertation on "Mexican Emigration to the United States, 1910–1930" (University of California, Berkeley, 1957) is the only general history of the first exodus. An offset copy of this objective, documented account is available via R & E Associates of San Francisco. Still in preparation are such other emigration studies as the cooperative history of Mexican labor migration, 1900–1970, directed by Arthur F. Corwin of the University of Connecticut.

After McWilliams there was no significant publication of historical interest on Mexican migration until economist Leo Grebler's monograph on twentieth-century *Mexican Immigration to the United States: The Record and Its Implications* (Graduate School of Business Administration, UCLA, 1966). This study, primarily statistical, also contains information on U.S. immigration law and procedures. It is partly incorporated into the final product of the Ford-funded Mexican American Study Project, *The Mexican-American People*, edited by Grebler and others. Another striking fact is that there are no published histories tracing the development of U.S. immigration policy toward Mexico; nor are there analyses on American attitudes toward Mexican emigration, although there are many works, published and unpublished, which can partly fulfill this purpose.[20] Moreover, no scholarly studies have yet been

---

19 "The Cultural Background of the Mexican Immigrant," *Rural Sociology*, VIII (1948), 239–255, is but one of several articles by Humphrey on the background of migration to industrial cities like Detroit. Missionary McLean, *That Mexican! As He Really Is, North and South of the Rio Grande* (New York, 1928), considers the transborder heritage of Juan García, a typical migrant worker and his family. Another missionary, Vernon McCombs, in *From Over the Border: A Study of Mexicans in the United States* (New York, 1926; reprinted by R & E Associates, 1970), emphasized social-rescue opportunities.

20 See, for example, the Grebler monograph and government publications that review precedents and practices related to Mexican labor migration. Among the latter are "The Immigration and Naturalization System of the United States," 81 Cong., 2 sess., *Sen. Rept. 1515* (1950); see also Roy L. Garis's detailed account of *Immigration Restriction: A Study of the Opposition to the Regulation of Immigration to the United States* (Macmillan, 1927), and historian Robert A. Divine's *American Immigration Policy, 1924–1952* (Yale University Press, 1957). There are also several master's theses concerned with debates on Mexican labor migration. See, for example, Ethel

printed on the U.S. Border Patrol, although there is one informal history available.[21]

Possibly two-thirds of all Mexicans who settled in the United States since 1917 originally entered without complying with immigration laws. The long standing need for an historical account of illegal migration from Mexico has been partly met by Julian Samora's *Los Mojados: The Wetback Story* (University of Notre Dame Press, 1971), a socio-economic analysis dealing primarily with the period since World War II. Although many migrants later legalized their status, often with the help of employers and immigrant-aid societies, wetbackism, as Richard Vásquez makes dramatically clear in his novel, *Chicano* (Doubleday and Co., 1970), has hung like a cloud over many Mexican barrios in the United States. Fear of *la migra* has been a way of life for Mexican families, and it has undoubtedly influenced the shaping of introverted "little Mexicos," the "invisible minority" phenomenon, and Chicano militancy. No one has yet studied this subject in depth, although Stan Steiner's journalistic account of *La Raza* (1969) indicates how important it is to an understanding of Chicano politics today. Nor has any historian or social scientist studied in depth the relation between illicit immigration and the passive resistance of Mexican settlers to naturalization or contact with certain civil and public agencies, a phenomenon that again suggests similarities between forbidden Chinese immigration and lying low in "China Town."[22] Also, there is no published account of political and religious refugees from Mexico during the period, 1900–1930, and their subcultural influence in such strategic southwestern cities as San Antonio, El Paso, and Los Angeles. And to date there is only one serious history of

---

M. Morrison, "A History of Recent Legislative Proposals Concerning Mexican Immigration" (University of Southern California, 1929); Joe W. Neal, "The Policy of the United States Toward Immigration from Mexico" (University of Texas, 1941); Dean L. Williams, "Some Political and Economic Aspects of Mexican Immigration into the United States since 1941, with Particular Reference to This Immigration into the State of California" (University of California, Los Angeles, 1950); and Robert J. Lipschultz, "American Attitudes toward Mexican Immigration, 1924–1952" (University of Chicago, 1962).

21 *The Border Wardens* (Prentice Hall, 1971), by John M. Myers, a writer of western Americana, is a popular but informative account of border control problems based on interviews and years of first-hand knowledge about the borderlands.

22 Among studies that probe Mexican resistance to naturalization, see Helen Walker, "Mexican Immigrants and American Citizenship," *Sociology and Social Research*, XIII (1929), 465–471; and Emory S. Bogardus, *The Mexican in the United States* (University of Southern California, 1934; reprinted by Arno, 1970).

Mexican repatriation by a North American scholar, namely, Abraham Hoffman's "The Repatriation of Mexican Nationals from the United States during the Great Depression," a study which makes extensive use of materials in the U.S. National Archives and in private collections. Prepared in 1970 as a doctoral dissertation at the University of California, Los Angeles, this study will be published by the University of Arizona Press in 1973. A Chicano study on repatriados in the 1930s, though announced by the Mexican-American Cultural Center, UCLA, has not yet made its appearance.

There is, moveover, an obvious need for incisive studies in historical demography. Only then will we obtain more satisfactory answers to the questions: How many people came from Mexico? How many stayed? The work of Taylor and Grebler, as well as Hoffman's incisive critique, "Mexican Repatriation Statistics: Some Suggested Alternatives to Carey McWilliams," *Western Historical Quarterly,* III (1972), 391–404, have indicated the statistical problems, not the least of which is the lack of firm figures on the ebb and flow of illegal migration over the border.

To date there is no satisfactory published bibliography or guide, in English or Spanish, specifically concerned with modern Mexican migration to the United States. However, the members of the Border Study Project, directed by sociologist Julian Samora of Notre Dame University, are preparing an extensive compilation of primary and secondary sources on trans-border labor. In addition, there is Arthur F. Corwin's introductory study, "Mexican Migration History: Literature and Research," *Latin American Research Review,* VIII (Summer 1973), 3–24.

The early history of Mexican labor in the United States is relatively well known, thanks to perceptive social scientists whose work we have previously acknowledged. Equally important, social scientists, particularly agricultural economists like Paul S. Taylor and Varden Fuller, have placed Mexican labor in a broad conceptual framework whereby one can readily visualize the historical function of imported waves of Chinese, Japanese, Filipino, Hindu, and Mexican labor in facilitating the development of big-scale California agriculture since the late nineteenth century.[23]

---

23 See "Historical Background of California's Farm Labor," *Rural Sociology,* I (1936), 281–295, coauthored by Taylor and Tom Vasey; and a major but little known historical study by Fuller that was published in the La Follette Committee hearings as "The Study of Agricultural Labor as a Factor in the Evolution of Farm Organiza-

Carey McWilliams made use of the foregoing perspectives in his *Factories in the Field: The Story of Migratory Farm Labor in California* (Little, Brown, 1939; reprinted by Peregrine Press, 1971). This work is a penetrating account of the rise of agribusiness empires which are almost unique to California. McWilliams' main theme here was capitalist exploitation of "cheap labor," including Orientals, poor whites, Mexicans, and others, and the related unionization struggles and racial tensions as they emerged in the period, 1910–1940. *Factories,* together with McWilliams' *Ill Fares the Land: Migrant and Migratory Labor in the United States* (Little, Brown, 1942; reprinted by Barnes and Noble, 1967), his *California: The Great Exception* (Current Books, 1949; reprinted by Greenwood Press, 1970), and his *North from Mexico,* provides a sweeping socialist interpretation of corporate capitalism, labor exploitation, and union-busting. The main focus of these works is California, but the analytical framework could be applied, with some reservations, to plantation-type agriculture systems found in such locales as the cotton belt of the Rio Grande Valley, the beet-fields of the Middle West, and the sugar fields of Hawaii and Puerto Rico. Only a few historical studies have fixed on the remarkable mobility of Mexican labor. George O. Coalson's doctoral dissertation on "The Development of the Migratory Farm Labor System in Texas, 1900–1954" (University of Oklahoma, 1955) has not yet been published, nor have other dissertations that provide historical perspectives. Moreover, monographs on Mexican labor in mines and railroads are virtually nonexistent.[24] Unionized labor is also a subject that holds special interest for such ethnic scholars as Juan Gómez-Quiñones and Ronald López, who seek deeper historical roots for Mexican labor militancy than the celebrated *huelga* of César Chávez.[25] Until the emergence of the ethnic studies movement, only a

tion in California," Senate Sub-Committee on Education and Labor, "Hearings on Violations of Free Speech and Rights of Labor," 76 Cong., 3 sess. (1940), 19777–19898.

[24] John C. Elac's M.A. thesis on "The Employment of Mexican Workers in U.S. Agriculture, 1900–1960: A Binational Economic Analysis" (University of California, Los Angeles, 1961) concentrates more on Mexican labor during the bracero program. Joseph F. Park's "The History of Mexican Labor in Arizona During the Territorial Period" (M.A. thesis, University of Arizona, 1961) is chiefly concerned with Mexican labor in mines. Histories of Mexican labor on the Southern Pacific and Santa Fe railroads have yet to be written.

[25] Some recent historical studies concerned with the unionization efforts of Mexican labor are Ronald W. López, "The El Monte Berry Strike of 1933," *Aztlán*, I (Spring 1970), 101–114; Charles Wollenberg's two articles, "Huelga, 1928 Style: The Imperial

few studies and reports dealt with Mexican and Mexican-American labor.[26]

No facet of Mexican labor has been more studied than the so-called bracero program, 1942–1964. Historians and social scientists have been attracted to the subject, partly because bi-national agreements were heatedly debated on both sides, and in part because much literature is available. See, for example, the impressive list of materials in English compiled by Beatriz Mass Gil, *Bibliografía de trabajadores mexicanos a los Estados Unidos* (Departamento de Estudios Económicos, Biblioteca del Banco de México, mimeographed, 1959). One of the first studies, *A History of the Emergency Farm Labor Supply Program, 1943–1947* (Agricultural Monograph No. 13, U.S. Department of Agriculture, mimeographed, 1951), by Wayne D. Rasmussen, covers the war-time origins of bi-national agreements. *Merchants of Labor: The Mexican Bracero Story* (McNally & Loftin, 1964), by Ernesto Galarza, combines historical method, field work, and many years of first-hand experience to produce an outstanding account of imported labor in California agriculture. Another important monograph is Richard B. Craig's *The Bracero Program: Interest Groups and Foreign Policy* (University of Texas Press, 1971), a near-exhaustive study of published literature on the politics of the program. Of related interest are incisive articles by Ellis W. Hawley, Charles M. Hardin, and others on pressure groups and perennial renewal of what was originally a tempor-

---

Valley Cantaloupe Worker's Strike," *Pacific Historical Review*, XXXVIII (1969), 45–48, and "Race and Class in Rural California: El Monte Berry Strike of 1933," *California Historical Quarterly*, LI (1972), 155–164; Harvey A. Levenstein, *Labor Organizations in the United States and Mexico: A History of Their Relations* (Greenwood Press, 1971); and Juan Gómez-Quiñones, "The First Steps: Chicano Labor Conflict and Organizing, 1900–1920," *Aztlán*, III (Spring 1972), 13–49.

26 Useful studies on Mexican and Mexican-American labor by Selden Menefee, Ernesto Galarza, Fred H. Schmidt, Walter Fogel, Lamar B. Jones, Robert C. Landholt, and many others can be found in such bibliographies as Mitchell Slobodek, *A Selective Bibliography of California Labor History* (Institute of Industrial Relations, UCLA, 1964), an annotated work that covers all ethnic groups during the period, 1873–1963; Isao Fujimoto and Jo Claire Shieffer, *Guide to Sources on Agricultural Labor* (Department of Applied Behavioral Sciences, University of California, Davis, mimeographed, 1969), an annotated guide suggesting important materials in government and non-government agencies. David C. Ruesink and Brice T. Batson, *Bibliography Relating to Agricultural Labor* (Agricultural Experiment Station, Texas A & M University, College Station, 1969), a non-annotated list of over a thousand items, including bibliographies and unpublished materials produced in period, 1964–1969; and Paul S. Taylor, "California's Farm Labor: A Review," *Agricultural History*, XLII (1968), 49–54, that suggests source materials gathered by congressional committees and the Federal Writers Project (WPA).

ary, war-time measure.[27] Other articles by Otey Scruggs, the Gilmores, and George O. Coalson trace the evolution of bracero use in Texas and California and survey some of the diplomatic problems involved.[28]

The wetback threat to the bracero program is considered by several writers of outstanding dissertations on Mexican contract labor, including John P. Carney, Robert D. Tomasek, and Johnny M. McCain.[29] Also valuable are Carrol Norquest's *Rio Grande Wetbacks: Mexican Migrant Workers* (University of New Mexico Press, 1972), a study that contains the revealing reminiscences of a Texas employer of wetbacks; and Scruggs, "The United States, Mexico and the Wetbacks, 1942–1947," *Pacific Historical Review*, XXX (1961), 149–164. In addition, many government publications contain historically-valuable information on contract labor and the problem of illegal entry.

Although numerous writers have covered facets of the bracero labor programs, there is not yet an historical analysis of the influence of contract-labor programs on immigration, legal and illegal, to the United States. Furthermore, there is no history of the commuters who work along the southwestern border and reside in Mexico. There are, however, some published items that trace this peculiar arrangement to the 1920s. Among them are "Commuters, Historical Background and Legal Challenges," in *Report of the Select Commission on Western Hemisphere Immigration* (Washington,

---

27 Ellis W. Hawley, "The Politics of the Mexican Labor Issue, 1950–1965," *Agricultural History*, XL (1966), 157–176; and Charles M. Hardin, "The Politics of Agriculture in the United States," *Journal of Farm Economics*, XXXII (1950), 571–581.

28 Some early precedents of the bracero program are examined by Scruggs in "The First Farm Labor Program, 1917–1921," *Arizona and the West*, II (1960), 319–326; and "Evolution of the Mexican Farm Labor Agreement of 1942," *Agricultural History*, XXXIV (1961), 140–149. The same author has written about Mexico's attempts to blacklist the use of braceros in Texas. See, for example, "Texas, Good Neighbor?" *Southwestern Social Science Quarterly*, XLIII (1963), 118–125; see also N. Ray Gilmore and Gladys W. Gilmore, "The Bracero in California," *Pacific Historical Review*, XXXII (1963), 263–282, a survey of the period 1917 to 1963, but principally since World War II; and a similar study by George O. Coalson, "Mexican Contract Labor in American Agriculture," *Southwestern Social Sceince Quarterly*, XXXIII (1952), 228–238.

29 John P. Carney, "Postwar Mexican Migration, 1945–1955, with Particular Reference to the Policies and Practices Concerning Its Control" (University of Southern California, 1957); Robert D. Tomasek, "The Political and Economic Implications of Mexican Labor in the United States under the Non-Quota System, Contract Labor Program and Wetback Movement" (University of Michigan, 1958); and Johnny M. McCain, "Contract Labor as a Factor in United States-Mexican Relations, 1942–1947" (University of Texas, 1970).

D.C., 1968), 99–130, and an extensive report by David S. North.[30]
Despite the availability of McWilliams' works and several dozen
sweeping surveys engendered by the ethnic studies movement, the
social history of twentieth-century Mexican Americans is still to be
written. The most important of the ethnic surveys to date, namely,
the aforementioned *The Mexican-American People: The Nation's
Second Largest Minority* (1970), by Leo Grebler *et al.*, is in many
ways an excellent assessment of contemporary social conditions, but
it suffers from a lack of historical perspective. There were no historians among the principal collaborators. It may also be noted that
some of the contributers to that extensive reconnaissance, like Nancie L. Gónzalez and Joan Moore, have published their own monographs on Mexican-American groups.[31] The would-be researchers
of Mexican-American social history would find the pioneer studies
of Gamio, Taylor, and others, and the immense social concern literature of missionaries, social reformers, health workers, and educators to be basic sources.[32] Sociologist Ellwyn R. Stoddard, for one,
has tapped such sources in his overview of the social and organiza-
tional development of *Mexican Americans* (Random House, 1973).
This latter work is a notable attempt to integrate Mexico's traumatic social history, border proximity, and historical periodization
into sociological analysis.

---

30 David S. North and others, *The Border Crossers, People Who Live in Mexico and
Work in the United States* (Washington, Transcentury Corporation, mimeographed,
1970). For other studies on commuters, see North's bibliography, 283–290.

31 Anthropologist Nancie L. González published *The Spanish Americans of New
Mexico: A Heritage of Pride* (University of New Mexico Press; rev. ed., 1969). This
study serves to update a moving report by George I. Sánchez on the isolated Hispano
folk of northern New Mexico. (*Forgotten People: A Study of New Mexicans* [University
of New Mexico Press, 1940; reprinted by Calvin Horn, 1969]). Sociologist Joan Moore,
with Alfredo Cuellar, published a survey on *Mexican Americans* (1971) in the Prentice-
Hall series on American ethnic minorities.

32 Emory Bogardus, in particular, would probably deserve a special place in any
social history of Mexican settlers in the United States. He published several sympathetic but not profound studies on Mexican acculturation problems, including *The
Mexican in the United States*. Among the articles by Bogardus the most significant
are perhaps those that have attempted to measure the degree of social acceptance and
assimilation. See, for example, "Second Generation Mexicans," *Sociology and Social
Research*, XIII (1929) 276–283; or "Racial Distance Changes in the United States during the Past Thirty Years," *ibid.*, XLIV (1959), 127–135, in which the author compares
data from 1926, 1946, and 1956, and finds that after World War II the status of Mexican Americans rose markedly. Also, see Manuel Servín's account of social retardation,
"The Pre-World War II Mexican American: An Interpretation," *California Historical Society Quarterly*, VL (1966), 325–338.

Materials for the social history of Mexican-descent groups in the United States can
be found in Bogardus' annotated "Literature and Research on Mexicans and Mexican-

The sense of social transition from migrant worker to Mexican-American settler and of the growing strain between the older immigrant generations and their American-born children can be appreciated in a rare autobiographical account by a Mexican immigrant, namely, Ernesto Galarza's *Barrio Boy* (University of Notre Dame Press, 1971), and a growing literature on social realism by such Mexican-American novelists as José A. Villarreals, *Pocho* (Doubleday, 1958; reprinted, 1970); Raymond Barrio, *The Plum Plum Pickers* (Ventura Press, 1969; reprinted by Canfield Press, 1971); and Richard Vásquez, *Chicano* (Doubleday, 1970). The social historian could also use significant community studies of an anthropological nature by Ruth Tuck (1946), Beatrice Griffith (1948), Pauline Kibbe (1946), Lyle Saunders (1954), Munro S. Edmonson (1957), William Madsen (1964), Arthur Rubel (1966), Margaret Clark (1959), and surveys by John H. Burma (1954) and Julian Samora (1966).[33] Although most of these studies are today sharply criticized by Chicano scholars, they nevertheless contain much important empirical data that cannot be entirely ignored.[34]

Given the present direction of Mexican-American studies and the emphasis on acculturation, we should know more about the twentieth-century patterns of *barrio* settlement near border towns, employment centers, or near such pre-established colonies as those in San Antonio, Los Angeles, or even Chicago.[35] Also, little is known

Americans," in his *The Mexicans in the United States*, 99–123. This compilation is supplemented by Robert C. Jones' non-annotated *Mexicans in the United States: A Bibliography* (Pan American Union, 1942). George I. Sánchez and Howard Putnam, *Materials Relating to the Education of Spanish-Speaking People in the United States: An Annotated Bibliography* (Austin, University of Texas Institute of Latin American Studies, 1959), suggests materials, including unpublished dissertations, for the history of educational, social, and health work among the Spanish-speaking, particularly in Texas.

33 These works can be found in bibliographies developed for Mexican-American studies.

34 The "stereotypes" projected by Anglo-American social scientists are critically analyzed and rejected, for example, by anthropologist Octavio I. Romano, in "The Anthropology and Sociology of Mexican Americans: The Distortion of Mexican-American History," *El Grito*, II (Fall 1968), 13–26; and in a bibliographic commentary by Nick C. Vaca, "The Mexican-American in the Social Sciences, 1912–1970, Part I: 1912–1935," *ibid.*, III (Spring 1970), 3–24, and "Part II: 1936–1970," *ibid.*, IV (Fall 1970), 17–51.

35 A useful model for settlement studies could be Taylor's *A Mexican-American Frontier, Nueces County, Texas* (1934), previously cited. The growing interest by Chicano historians in settlement patterns and urbanization is indicated by Albert M. Camarillo in "Chicano Urban History: A Study of Compton's Barrio, 1936–1970," *Aztlán*, II (Fall 1971), 79–106.

about social service agencies and the extent to which they may have attracted refugee and migrant families to settle on the U.S. side, or may have served as a subsidy for employers and the migrant-labor subculture. Likewise, little history has been written about twentieth-century Protestant or Catholic missions among Mexican migrant workers and settlers.[36] Nor, despite the outpourings of literature on educational efforts among the Spanish-speaking inhabitants of the Southwest, is there a satisfactory history of this subject.[37] Furthermore, although materials abound, no worthwhile history has yet been published about the inflammatory topic of race relations.[38]

Conceivably, history could be written about Mexican-American folklore and the persistence of subcultural traits, but historical writing about art and literature which is distinctly Mexican American would seem premature at this time. In the future, however, it may be possible to write about the rise of social protest art and literature as exemplified in *El Grito, Con Safos,* the Teatro Campesino, in syllabi like *The Chicanos: Mexican American Voices,* edited by Ed Ludwig and James Santibañez (Penguin Books, 1971), and in similar works. Someday, one might also do a historical appraisal of the emerging Mexican-American novel, particularly that which portrays adjustment problems of Mexican settlers and labor conditions. Other possibilities in cultural history are indicated by the

---

36 Some denominational histories of evangelical work among Spanish-speaking groups have been written by non-professionals; see, for example, David H. Stratton, *The First Century of Baptists in New Mexico, 1849–1950* (Albuquerque, Woman's Missionary Union of New Mexico, 1954).

37 Pioneer educators have described the lamentable educational conditions among certain Mexican-American groups. See, for example, Hershel T. Manuel, *The Spanish-Speaking Children of the Southwest—Their Education and Public Welfare* (University of Texas Press, 1965); and George I. Sánchez, "History, Culture and Education," in Samora, ed., *La Raza: Forgotten Americans,* 1–26. Thomas P. Carter, a student of Sánchez, has published a social indictment entitled *Mexican Americans in School: A History of Educational Neglect* (New York, College Entrance Board, 1970).

38 See, for instance, anthropologist Lyle Saunders' *A Guide to Materials Bearing on Cultural Relations in New Mexico* (University of New Mexico Press, 1944), a partly annotated survey that covers the major ethnic groups, namely Indians, Hispanos, and Anglos, in an area broader than New Mexico. Materals for the history of race relations in southern California are indicated by Ruth Riemer in *An Annotated Bibliography of Materials on Ethnic Problems* (Haynes Foundation and Department of Sociology and Anthropology, UCLA, mimeographed, 1947). See also Charles Wollenberg, *et al., Ethnic Conflict in California History* (Los Angeles, Tinnon-Brown, Inc., 1970), an overview; Robert F. Heizer and Alan J. Almquist, *The Other Californians: Prejudice and Discrimination under Spain, Mexico and the United States to 1920* (University of California Press, 1970), a superficial work; and Carolyn Zeleny, "Relations between the Spanish Americans and Anglo-Americans in New Mexico" (Ph.D. dissertation, Yale University, 1944), an anthropological treatment.

publication of a massive dissertation on *La lengua española en la historia de California* (Madrid, Ediciones Cultura Hispánica, 1971), written by Antonio Blanco S., a Spaniard who has taught Hispanic languages in Mexico and in southern California universities.

In recent years a gush of books and articles by such writers as John G. Dunne, Peter Mathiessen, Peter Nabokov, Michael Jenkinson, Richard M. Gardner, Patricia B. Blawis, Frances L. Swadesh, to mention only some, have told the story of Crystal City, La Huelga, the land-grant struggle in New Mexico, and other facets of Mexican-American militancy and the civil-rights movement. But scarcely any of these works can be classified as political history. Moreover, the few studies by political scientists and anthropologists that have attempted to analyze the political condition or behavior of Mexican-American groups scarcely go beyond a brief comment on the passivity and Mexico-style patronage that characterize the Spanish-speaking enclaves in northern New Mexico and south Texas.[39] With one or two exceptions, like Jack E. Holmes's penetrating account of *Politics in New Mexico* (University of New Mexico Press, 1967) which contains some historical background material on the political behavior of Hispano groups in New Mexico, there are virtually no political histories of Spanish-surnamed peoples in the modern Southwest. And yet recent studies suggest that there is indeed much history that could be written about the political past of such Mexican-American groups as the LULACS, founded in the 1920s, and about political leaders like Alonso Perales, George I. Sánchez, and Dennis Chávez.[40]

Sensing the drama and significance of border conflict, many historians of the Southwest (like J. F. Rippy, Charles Cumberland, and Walter P. Webb) originally trained in the Bolton or Hackett schools of southwestern history and many freelance or professional writers (like Paul Horgan and Clarence C. Clendenen) have been attracted to the subject of United States-Mexico territorial and border re-

---

39 An example would be the previously mentioned *The Spanish Americans of New Mexico*, by Nancie L. González.

40 For example, Robin F. Scott, "The Mexican American in the Los Angeles Area, 1920–1950: From Acquiescence to Activity" (M.A. thesis, University of Southern California, 1971), finds that World War II was a turning point toward political activism. Charles R. Chandler, "The Mexican-American Protest Movement in Texas" (Ph.D. dissertation, Tulane University, 1968), also traces the emergence of civic and political-action groups from World War II.

lations.[41] Unquestionably, Anglo-Mexican border conflicts have influenced the whole gamut of race relations in the Southwest, especially in the Texas border region which historically has functioned as the main channel of Mexican migration by stages to the United States. But, with one or two exceptions, there have been no serious efforts by historians to interpret the influence of border confrontation on the development of race consciousness and on those "stereotypes" of greasers, gringos, gabachos, anglos, pochos, chicanos, meskins, rinches, la migra, and the like.[42]

Historians interested in border settlement should note that there is a fund of information and perspectives of historical value in the publications of geographers, demographers, economists, and sociologists.[43] Nor should works by folklorists and professional writers be overlooked.[44]

In recent years research has been promoted by the established centers for Latin American studies in border universities and by the development of institutional cooperation among border educational institutions.[45] In addition, the Notre Dame "Border Study

41 See, for example, Robert D. Gregg, *The Influence of Border Troubles on Relations Between the United States and Mexico, 1876–1910* (Johns Hopkins University Press, 1937; reprinted by DaCapo Press, 1970); William A. Hager, "The Plan of San Diego, Unrest on the Texas Frontier in 1915," *Arizona and the West*, V (1963), 327–336; Ben H. Proctor, "The Modern Texas Rangers: A Law Enforcement Dilemma in the Rio Grande Valley," in John A. Carroll, ed., *Reflections of Western Historians* (University of Arizona Press, 1969), 215–233; Sheldon B. Liss, *A Century of Disagreement: The Chamizal Conflict 1864–1964* (Washington, D.C., University Press, 1965); and Norris Hundley, *Dividing the Waters: A Century of Conflict Between the United States and Mexico* (University of California Press, 1966). A work that suggests the great range of literature on border topics and research possibilities for historians and social scientists is the late Charles C. Cumberland's major bibliographical essay on *The United States-Mexico Border: A Selective Guide to the Literature* which appeared as a supplement to *Rural Sociology*, XXV (June 1960).

42 Among recent works, Acuña's *Occupied America* shows the keenest awareness of the impact of border animosities on racial attitudes. See also sociologist S. Dale McLemore's structural analysis of "The Origins of Mexican American Subordination in Texas," *Social Science Quarterly* LIII (1973), 656–671.

43 Some examples are Richard L. Nostrand, "The Hispano-American Borderlands: A Regional, Historical Geography" (University of California, Los Angeles, 1968), an outstanding doctoral dissertation; and D. W. Meinig, *Southwest: Three Peoples in Geographical Change* (Oxford University Press, 1971), a broad interpretation of Indian, white, and Hispano relations on cultural and economic frontiers.

44 Two relevant examples are Haldeen Braddy, *Mexico and the Old Southwest: People, Palaver and Places* (Kennikat Press, 1971), a miscellany of folktale, border lingo, smuggling, and revolutionary troubles; and Ovid Demaris, *Poso del Mundo: Inside the Mexican American Border from Tijuana to Matamoros* (Little, Brown and Co., 1970), an exposé of border corruption and the problems of border development.

45 The Texas Western Press at the University of Texas, El Paso, publishes a mono-

Project" is presently investigating such topics as labor, community organization, law enforcement, social and religious agencies, and other facets of border subcultures. Out of this project has emerged Samora's previously mentioned *Los Mojados* (1971).

Mexican historians have written eloquently about United States-Mexico relations, and, in particular, about the events that culminated in the territorial dismemberment of 1848.[46] Also, there are countless histories of events, forces, and personalities that shaped the Mexican people.[47] But Mexican scholars have written practically nothing of an historical nature about mass emigration to the United States, and not much more about the condition of Mexican nationals and their descendants in North American society.[48] It is interesting to note that the only major research studies on Mexican emigration by a Mexican writer, namely those by Manuel Gamio, were published not in Spanish but in English by the University of Chicago Press under the titles of *Mexican Immigration* (1930) and *The Mexican Immigrant* (1931).

Until 1940 Mexican literature had been "officially concerned" with the problems generated by mass emigration, that is, depopulation, loss of labor, and the responsibility keenly felt by the revolutionary government either to repatriate or protect Mexican

graph series that includes such useful works as John Haddox, *Los Chicanos: An Awakening People* (1970). The Border State-Consortium for Latin America, consisting of the Universities of Arizona and New Mexico, California State University, San Diego, and the University of Texas, El Paso, has initiated a series of occasional papers edited by the Inter-American Institute of the latter university. These papers are concerned with all aspects of border studies. See Ellwyn Stoddard's two essays, *Comparative United States-Mexico Border Studies* (Occasional Paper No. 1, Border State Consortium for Latin America, University of Texas, El Paso, 1970), and "The United States-Mexico Border as a Research Laboratory," *Journal of Inter-American Studies*, II (1969), 477–488.

46 For example, Carlos Bosch García, *Historia de las relaciones entre Mexico y los Estados Unidos, 1819–1848* (México, UNAM, 1961), an objective, carefully researched account of American Manifest Destiny and territorial conflict by a Spanish-immigrant scholar of distinguished reputation.

47 Works by distinguished historians like Lucas Alamán, Justo Sierra, Silvio Zavala, and Daniel Cosío Villegas are found in Luís González, *Fuentes de la historia contemporánea de México: libros y folletos* (3 vols., México, El Colegio de México, 1961–1962). Another important bibliography is Roberto Ramos, *Bibliografía de la Revolución Mexicana* (3 vols., México, Secretaría de Relaciones Exteriores, 1931–1940). See also a handy bibliographical essay on Mexican history by Charles C. Cumberland, *Mexico, the Struggle for Modernity* (Oxford University Press, 1968), 334–365.

48 Mario Gil's *Nuestros Buenos Vecinos* (México, Editorial Azteca, 1964) is an historical condemnation of "Yanqui" imperialism that covers territorial loss, border conflicts, and touches on the plight of Mexican groups which remained in the Southwest after the territorial cession. *Los Estados Unidos y el México olvidado* (México, Costa-Amic, 1970), by Agustin Cue Cánovas, deals with similar themes.

workers in the United States. The writers were usually government and consular personnel or economists and demographers like Santibañez, Landa y Piña, Loyo, and Hidalgo.[49]

Although the Mexican government has for more than a half-century sought to repatriate Mexican nationals from the United States, there is still no published study of these efforts. Nevertheless, despite the few Mexican works directly concerned with migratory flows, there are some impressive publications by such scholars as Moisés T. de la Peña and Moisés González Navarro that bear on the causes of the campesino exodus up to 1929.[50] Many other studies by both Mexican and North American authors describing a range of agrarian conditions in Mexico could serve as historical background to Mexican emigration.[51]

The historian of the Mexican-American heritage should also note that some light is cast on the rural origins of certain southwestern *barrios* and *colonias* by studies of Mexico's Indo-peasant communities. Among the more pertinent are the works of Robert Redfield, Oscar Lewis, George Foster, Eric Wolf, and Lola B. Schwartz, and by Mexico's Gonzálo Aguirre Beltrán, Ricardo Pozas, and Julio de la Fuente. Nor should the ethnic historian ignore a genre of literature which could be called the "psychic history" of La Raza. It includes the works of such provocative analysts of national character as Samuel Ramos, Octavio Paz, Leopoldo Zea, Rogelio Díaz Guerrero, Santiago Ramírez, and Francisco González Pineda. Some of this literature and its historical significance is discussed by John L. Phelan in "México y lo Mexicano," *Hispanic American Historical Review*, XXXVI (1956), 309–318.

---

49 Mexican writings on emigration are more fully covered by Arthur F. Corwin in "Historia de la emigración mexicana, 1900–1970: literatura é investigación," *Historia Mexicana*, XXII (1972), 188–220.

50 See, for example, Moisés T. de la Peña, "Problemas demográficos y agrarios," in *Problemas agrícolas é industriales de México*, II (Julio–Diciembre de 1950), 9–327; and two studies by Moisés González Navarro, *La Colonización en México, 1877–1910* (México, Talleres Estampillas y Valeres, 1960), and "La política colonizadora del Porfiriato," *Estudios Históricos Americanos* (El Colegio de México, 1953), 183–239.

51 Among the earliest such works are Andrés Molina Enríquez' cry for land reform, *Los grandes problemas nacionales* (México, 1909), and geographer George M. McBrides's *The Land Systems of Mexico* (American Geographical Society, 1923; reprinted by Octogon Books, 1971). Other significant examples would be Nathan Whetten's *Rural Mexico* (University of Chicago Press, 1948; reprinted, 1964), and historian John Womack's *Zapata and the Mexican Revolution* (Knopf, 1968). The latter two studies suggest many other sources for the study of agrarian conditions and revolutionary unrest. Also, see Jorge Martínez Rios, *Tenencia de la tierra y desarrollo agrario en México: Bibliografía selectiva y comentada, 1522–1968* (México, Instituto de Investigaciones Sociales, UNAM, 1970).

The sensitive nature of the bi-national bracero agreements and the administrative problems faced by both governments churned up countless comments on *bracerismo* in Mexican newspapers, periodicals, government reports, and academic dissertations.[52] And yet no Mexican writer to date has published an historical account of the bracero program, "wetbackism," or the sudden rise in legal immigration to the United States beginning in the 1950s.

Neglect of Mexican groups in the United States by Mexican writers can in part be explained by a xenophobic nationalism that tended to regard "expatriates" merely as a shameful example of revolutionary failure, or that tended to discount Mexican nationals across the border as *vendepatrias, pochos,* or *malinchistas,* or simply unfortunates who unwittingly had sold their Mexican birthright for Anglo gold.[53] The situation has changed, however, and there is now a rising demand for studies centered on Mexican-descent groups in the United States. For one thing, increasing publicity has been given in Mexican newspapers and other periodicals to La Raza militancy in the southwestern states, or the "lost territories." For another, hundreds of young Chicanos who have made the pilgrimage back to *la madre patria,* privately or on U.S. fellowships, to study cultural heritage in Mexican academic institutions, have aroused an interest in their Mexican instructors who now feel they need to know more about the Mexican subculture in the United States. Furthermore, Mexico now has well-funded research centers like El Colegio de México and the Instituto de Investigaciones Sociales, UNAM, and a growing number of fulltime historians and social scientists who can respond to demands for more information about Mexican-descent groups over the border. In addition, the Mexican and United States governments have recently agreed to

---

52 Some examples are José Lázaro Salinas, *La emigración de braceros* (León, México, Imprenta Cuauhtemoc, 1955), an analysis of the causes of the bracero exodus and a proposal for reforming the contracting system; and Stella Leal Carrillo, *Importancia económica y social de la población mexicana en Estados Unidos* (México, UNAM, 1963), an attempt to assess the economic importance of Mexican bracero and Mexican immigrant labor in the U.S. economy.

53 See, for example, Alfonso Fabila, *El problema de la emigración de obreros y campesinos mexicanos* (México, Talleres Graficos de la Nación, 1928), a tract distributed by the Mexican government that warned La Raza not to emigrate to the American El Dorado where it would most likely find itself the victim of discrimination, exploitation, and unbearable Americanization pressures in the public schools. Humberto Robles Arenas's *Los Desarraigados* (México, Instituto Nacional de Bellas Artes, 1962) is a play which dramatizes the mental anguish of Mexican immigrants who look on helplessly as their children reject their Mexican heritage.

study common border problems and the causes of massive illegal infiltration of Mexican nationals into the United States.[54]

Meanwhile, Mexican academics who have recently written about Mexican-descent groups in the United States seem to find themselves in the same stages of exploration and catharsis as many American ethnic writers. An example is Gilberto López y Riva's brief historical and sociological survey, *Los Chicanos: una minoría nacional explotada* (México, Editorial Nuestro Tiempo, 1971). López, who originally submitted this study for a degree in anthropology at the National University of Mexico, did no first-hand research, but instead borrowed heavily from McWilliams, the UCLA Mexican-American Study Project, and the literature produced by ethnic militants who have written popular and facile accounts of conquest, exploitation, and the genesis of the Raza movement.

Original research, however, is now being undertaken on such topics as emigration and repatriation by a number of young Mexican scholars associated with El Colegio de México.[55] Also, it is likely that a Mexican scholar will soon undertake a serious study of the impact of returning migrant workers on the pattern of economic and cultural development in Mexico. Thus far, this subject has scarcely been touched upon by Mexican writers, although it has caught the interest of such American writers as Richard Hancock and Howard L. Campbell.[56]

Another significant topic that may soon attract the attention of a Mexican or an American historian is the *Mexicanidad* and *La Raza* consciousness that for years has been sponsored by Mexican diplomatic personnel serving in the United States. Undoubtedly this has had a profound effect on the question of cultural identity and the

---

[54] Following talks between President Richard M. Nixon and President Luis Echeverría in Washington, D.C., during June 1972, the two countries appointed high-level study groups to prepare reports and make policy recommendations. Both governments believe that more than two million Mexicans may be illegally living in the United States. This information comes from personal interviews with Mexican consular officials, Washington, D.C., January 4–5, 1973.

[55] Historian Romeo Flores is presently investigating the previously unstudied subject of Mexican policy and attitudes toward the exodus of Mexican labor to the United States. Mercedes Carreras de Velasco, a graduate student in history, has completed an M.A. thesis on "La repatriación de Mexicanos, 1920–1940" (1973), which is written from the Mexican point of view.

[56] Richard Hancock, *The Role of the Bracero in the Economic and Cultural Dynamics of Mexico: A Case Study of Chihuahua* (Hispanic Amerian Society, Stanford University, 1959); and Howard L. Campbell, "Bracero Migration and the Mexican Economy, 1951–1964" (Ph.D. dissertation, American University School of International Service, 1972). Both works contain excellent bibliographies.

low naturalization rates that have characterized Mexican settlers in the United States, yet there is scarcely any published literature on the topic.

In summing up the present state of Mexican literature on Mexican-descent groups in the United States, it could be said that Gamio's *The Mexican Immigrant: His Life Story* (1931), translated and statistically updated to 1967 in a long prologue by demographer Gilberto Loyo and republished in Spanish as *El inmigrante Mexicano* (México, UNAM, 1969), is still the most important work of a scholarly nature in the Spanish language by a Mexican writer.

THE PRESENT STATE OF MEXICAN-AMERICAN ETHNIC HISTORY

Conceptual difficulties in Mexican-American history are nurtured by the coexistence of at least two distinct schools, each seeking to develop ethnic studies along diverging lines, and each counting many professional newcomers and preprofessionals among their numbers. In some cases both schools exist independently on the same campus. The one school, which seems more inclined toward the term "Mexican American," works within the traditional disciplines of history, anthropology, political science, and the like, and is controlled or accredited by the same. In the ethnic parlance of our times this might be called the "establishment school." The other school, which has a more uniform preference for the term "Chicano," is more oriented toward the barrio subculture and functions more like a semi-autonomous black-studies center, or the new "experimental colleges," but with a strictly-defined ethnic group determining curriculum content, teaching qualifications, and research priorities. This could be called the "La Raza school."

This dualism might seem to suggest that any evaluation of the present state of Mexican-American studies, including history, would require both an "establishment appraisal" and a "La Raza appraisal" by a spokesman from each school. However, since both schools are so new—dating no earlier than 1966—it would seem possible to apply the same academic standards of measurement to both of them, especially if one considers ethnic history only. Now if this history is pictured as a series of developmental stages then one might appraise the present state of this new-born academic vocation as follows:

The exploratory stage. Like ethnic studies in general much of the energy poured into the exploratory stage of Mexican-American history has so far been expended on certain quasi-political tasks. Some of these may be summarized as: providing a catharsis for minority groups by giving ethnic studies representation in the academic curriculum and by giving minority students a voice in ethnic studies; promoting ethnic pride, for example, by stressing ethnic contributions to national life, or, in a more militant form, by fostering cultural nationalism or racial separatism; erasing stereotypes about minorities in Anglo-American literature, for example, by challenging misleading impressions that migrant labor was docile labor, or that it posed an assimilation problem; developing various compensatory claims upon the national society for restoration of land grants, for preferential immigration laws, for bilingual and bicultural education, and the like; and educating, or indoctrinating, the general student body and the general public about the special status or condition of a minority as a prerequisite for political action or social reform.

The exploratory stage crackles with interscholastic controversy concerning preliminary objectives and methods. Speaking, we presume, for the "establishment school," historian Manuel A. Machado, Jr., in his "Mexican-American History: Problems and Prospects," *Western Review,* VIII (Winter 1971), 15–21, deplores, *con salsa picante,* the trend toward polarization, demogoguery, and counter-stereotyping that he feels only serves to abort a rational appreciation of the needs, functions, and place of ethnic history. Controversy is further illustrated by the hot discussion over beginning points. At present many ethnic specialists seem to have no fixed idea as to when Mexican-American minority history properly begins, or when one should date the birth of La Raza history. Joseph Navarro's article on historiographical needs, "The Condition of Mexican-American History," *Journal of Mexican-American History,* I (Fall 1970), 25–52, may be considered a statement from the Mexican-American school. Navarro would date relevant minority history from 1848. A post-doctoral fellow in history, Juan Gómez-Quiñones, presents what may be taken for a characteristic Raza interpretation in "Research Notes on the Twentieth Century," *Aztlán,* I (Spring 1970), 115–132. Gómez-Q. would date the political history of Chicanos from approximately 1900 when he first detects the emergence of a distinct Raza conscience and the first sparks of an emancipation struggle. Rodolfo Acuña, who conceives of Chicano history as an epic of alien conquest and colonialism, would date relevant history, if one were to judge by his *Occupied America* (1972), from the Anglo invasion of Texas.

On the other hand, there seems to be a general agreement that, in the broadest sense, Raza history begins before Columbus. Jesús Chavarría suggests, in "A Precis and a Tentative Bibliography on Chicano History," *Aztlán*, I (Spring 1970), 133–141, that since Chicanos are of Indian descent their cultural origins go back to pre-historical times. Robert P. Haro makes much the same point in "A Bibliographical Essay" that, again, reflects the Indian renaissance of the Mexican Revolution. The ancient but moribund cultures of Mexico, principally the Aztec, must be relearned by Chicanos, yet, typically, nothing is said about sources for the study of the living heritage of Spain.[57]

As previously indicated, one of the most notable statements thus far on concepts and time periods is Gómez-Quiñones' bibliographical article, "Toward a Perspective on Chicano History," *Aztlán*, II (Fall 1971), 1–49. The author would accept the relevancy of pre-Columbian beginnings, and he would acknowledge acculturative influences from both Mexico and the United States. But, like other Chicano spokesmen, anthropologist Octavio Romano for one, Gómez-Q. insists that Chicano communities have followed a line of distinctive development through an interplay of "a minority-territorial enclave" with larger national or imperial forces. Thus, La Raza should be studied within the framework of colonial relations and patterns. This being the case, the general history of the Chicano people would begin in 1598 with the first Hispano-Mexican settlement in what is now the American Southwest.

Given the foregoing examples, it is hardly surprising that most persons practicing Mexican-American history are still exploring purposes, methods, definitions, and the nature and scope of the subject matter. But in spite of absorption of energies by exploratory tasks, there is on most campuses of the Southwest a gradual progression towards a more disciplined, objective, and investigatory approach toward ethnic history. This dialectical progression is accom-

---

57 The essay by Haro, a specialist in Latin American acquisitions at the University of California Library, Davis, is one of the more impressive efforts by young Chicano writers. It may be found in *Con Safos*, II (1971), 50–59.

panied by an increasing recognition that no program of Mexican-American history, no matter how defined, can achieve its academic purposes unless there are more historical materials available.

The survey stage. Many specialists in Mexican-American or Raza history have struggled through the exploratory phase to find themselves immersed in the elementary task of developing history surveys and general reading lists. Unlike black history specialists who can draw upon a reservoir of general and specialized historical literature, historians of Mexican-American studies had little to start with except an undiscriminating mixture, so to speak, of political tracts, anthropological observations, and Carey McWilliams. Nevertheless, Mexican-American survey exercises have served some writers and editors to identify the most obvious gaps in the literature and to prepare some of the new survey texts mentioned in the first part of this article.

The documentary stage. Exploratory and survey tasks in a still nebulous field of historical endeavors have left little time for the location, identification, and classification of source materials in archives, special collections, and oral history projects. Still, as Mexican-American history becomes more institutionalized at the graduate level and better funded with fellowship support, and as eager young historians find their bearings through the mist of ethnic rhetoric, there will be an expanding search for more documentary sources and long forgotten dissertations.

At present the search for new documentation for Mexican-American history is being carried forward by graduate students and faculty members, mostly those associated with the "establishment school." Some random examples would be Carlos Cortés who has worked on Mexican settlement in the San Bernardino area with a Ford Foundation grant;[58] Lawrence Cardoso, University of Wyoming, who has searched in Mexico City archives for materials on the origins of Mexican emigration; José R. Juárez, University of California, Davis, presently working on documenting the relations between the Catholic church and Chicanos; Johnny M. McCain of San Antonio College who is studying Mexican labor settlement in the mecca of San Antonio; Manuel Servín of Arizona State University who is preparing a history of race prejudice in California;

---

[58] This project is described in "CHICOP: A Response to the Challenge of Local Chicano History," *Aztlán*, II (Fall 1970), 1–14.

and Américo Paredes and graduate students at the University of Texas Center for Mexican-American Studies, who are preparing a history of the Lower Rio Grande Valley.

The monographic stage. So far only a tiny harvest of published monographs has resulted from the search for new source materials. Leonard Pitt's *The Decline of the Californios* (1966) is a vanguard model of solid, objective research. *A Tragic Cavalier: Governor Manuel Salcedo of Texas, 1808–1813* (University of Texas Press, 1971), by Felix D. Almáraz, Jr., is another example of careful work in hitherto unused sources. And sociologist Julian Samora's *Los Mojados* (1971) is an example of a monograph that combines both historical and social-science methodology and materials.

The publication of research is not only receiving encouragement from a large number of commercial and university presses but also from the new ethnic journals, principally, *El Grito, A Journal of Contemporary Mexican-American Thought* (Quinto Sol Publications, Berkeley), a Chicano voice founded in 1968; *Aztlán, Chicano Journal of the Social Sciences and the Arts*, launched in the spring of 1970 by the Chicano Cultural Center, UCLA, with a projected monograph series on social science and history topics; and the *Journal of Mexican-American History*, founded at the University of California, Santa Barbara, in 1970 by a group of graduate students interested in developing a broader definition of Mexican-American history. In addition, a new *Journal of Ethnic Studies*, sponsored by Western Washington State College, Bellingham (Jeffrey D. Wilner, managing editor), invites contributions on all ethnic groups.[59] Moreover, journals specializing in Latin America (such as the *Latin American Research Review* and the *Journal of Inter-American Studies*), and those with a special interest in the Southwest (like *Journal of the West, Southwestern Historical Quarterly, Social Science Quarterly, Pacific Historical Review, Arizona and the West,* and *New Mexico Historical Review*), to name only a few, have welcomed original contributions based on monographic research in Mexican-American history.

Future stages. The creation of a large and respectable body of revisionist literature and revisionist schools in Mexican-American

---

[59] See, for example, a suggestive article by Abraham Hoffman on "Chicano History: Problems and Potentialities," which appeared in the *Journal of Ethnic Studies*, I (Spring 1973), 6–12. Professor Hoffman also contributed a number of suggestions to the present article.

history—such as now characterize the history of western expansion or Negro history—will be a long and arduous process. By revisionist literature we mean the work produced by professional historians who revise or debate the interpretations of other professional or reputable historians. The present outlook is that for some time to come the efforts of many Mexican-American and Raza scholars will be consumed by preliminary survey and monographic tasks. Yet some ethnic historians are already at work on advanced research fronts pushing back beginning points, rewriting the standard interpretations, and looking increasingly across the border to Mexican origins or to the forgotten enclaves of Hispano-Mexican folk. At the same time revisionist assumptions are being revised. There is a growing recognition of, if not appreciation for, the earlier works of North American and Mexican historians. In this sense the new ethnic history is merely a new phase of previously established disciplines. And McWilliams himself is coming under increasing critical evaluation by ethnic scholars. As young scholars have gained more awareness of complexities, some of the earlier simplistic premises have begun to fade, among them the ideas that the true history of the Southwest has been purposely suppressed or distorted by the Anglo establishment, or that La Raza was an abandoned child of the Anglo-American conquest of the Southwest.

Beyond the dialectics of revisionism there is the task of synthesis. The search widens for a more embracing theme that would pull together growing complexities and diverse geo-historical experiences—not fully considered by McWilliams—into one bundle called the Mexican-American heritage. Ideally, this bundle would contain the peon experience under Spanish feudalism and the proletarian experience under American corporate capitalism; the pioneer experience in frontier enclaves, and the La Raza experience in urban ghettos; the experience of those who have moved into the mainstream of national society, and the experience of those who remained on its margins, either as folk groups, or *mojados,* or "forgotten peoples."

Most textbook historians are still inclined to see a continuum between the Spanish frontier and the new Southwest that has been transformed by modern technology and labor mobility. And, as we have seen, some historians (particularly Raza historians) and some Chicano sociologists (Rodolfo Alvarez, for example) prefer a variant of this synthetic theme which sees native peoples under some continuous form of colonialism, whether Spanish, Mexican, or Anglo-American.[60] Publications thus far point to a long trajectory of efforts to establish the continuity of the Mexican-American experience. Obviously, the preparation of new syntheses that sum up and interpret the main facets of the Mexican-American past in a convincing manner must depend on a larger output of scholarly research. When this has been achieved, we shall see whether Mexican-American historians of any stripe can climb higher than did McWilliams with his *North from Mexico*. As it is, this primeval volume still stands as the closest approach to a philosophical or protean summary of Mexican-American history.

None of the foregoing observations mean to imply that there is a clean split between the two academic groups now engaged in producing Mexican-American history. Like drops of mercury ethnic scholars seem to run together, and even work together for some purposes, and run apart for others. Both schools are in fundamental accord that the history of Mexicans and their descendants in the Southwest has been neglected. But, whereas the "establishment school" would integrate this history into national history, the "La Raza school," which includes moderates as well as militants, would seek to develop, in Mexican terms, an exclusive history of *la pequeña patria*. Or, to paraphrase Abraham Lincoln, to create a "history of La Raza, by La Raza, and for La Raza." Yet, at the same time, it would be a history of justification aimed at larger audiences in both the United States and Mexico. It is likely that the two groups, loosely defined as they may be, will maintain separate identities and goals for a long time to come. In fact, this seems assured so long as public and private funding continue to support cultural pluralism in academic institutions.

---

[60] The effort by Alvarez to establish the unity and continuity of La Raza consciousness is based on the sweeping thesis that all waves of Mexican settlers in the Southwest since the Alamo have been inescapably conditioned by a preexisting structure of colonial conquest and caste discrimination. See his "The Psycho-Historical and Socio-Economic Development of the Chicano Community in the United States," *Social Science Quarterly*, LIII (1973), 920–942; and in an earlier version, *Social Science Quarterly*, LII (1971), 15–29. Sociologist Tomás Almaguer follows a similar line of conjecture in his "Toward the Study of Chicano Colonialism," *Aztlán*, II (Spring 1971), 7–21. One might here take note of Joan W. Moore's seminal article, "Colonialism: The Case of the Mexican Americans," *Social Problems*, XVII (1970), 463–471.

Mexican-American History: A Reply

Rodolfo Acuña

*The author is chairman of the Chicano studies depart-
ment at California State University, Northridge.*

ARTHUR F. CORWIN'S ARTICLE, "Mexican-American History: An
Assessment," is disturbing because it misleads the uninformed
reader as to the status and direction of Chicano history and studies.
Corwin shows almost no understanding of Chicano scholarship and
attempts to force Chicano history into a prescribed mold. Before
beginning my "assessment" of Corwin's "assessment," I would like
to make it clear that the conflict is not as simplistic as Corwin makes
it appear: it is not solely a white-brown difference, or academician
versus polemicist, but an attempt by one group to determine the
direction of the research and writings of another. In fact, revision-
istic historians, such as Howard Lamar, are much closer to the so-
called Chicano school than the "cowboy scholars" whom Corwin
attempts to emulate. In the interests of brevity, this rejoinder
focuses on two basic contradictions in the Corwin article: his use
of a double standard in assessing Chicano and Anglo-American
sources; and the political implications of his assessments.

At the core of Corwin's attack on Chicano-activist scholars is his
narrow application of the word *professional*. He seems to imply
that anyone who actively identifies with the aspirations of the Chicano community and advocates changes automatically forfeits his
right to synthesize objectively the history of that community. (If
Corwin's implication were carried to its logical conclusion, anything written on the United States by an Anglo-American would
be invalid.) Corwin evidently is confusing professionalism with
nativism, and is attempting to destroy a body of literature which

he considers alien or foreign to his prescribed views of the history of the region.

Corwin's introductory paragraph, on page 1, sets the tone for his assessment. He writes that Carey McWilliams was "a sort of Lone Ranger coming to the aid of a neglected people. . . ." While I agree with him in his commendation of McWilliams, I reject his overt paternalism and his insensitivity in glorifying a Texas Ranger, which is similar to praising a Storm Trooper to a Jew. Moreover, while Corwin praises McWilliams, he covertly attempts to discredit him: on page 2, Corwin attempts to show that Chicanos have erroneously based many of their conclusions on McWilliams's work. He attempts to disprove McWilliams's "frontier thesis" that "Mexicans since colonial times have migrated north over familiar land with little or no sense of changing frontiers." His authority is Walter Prescott Webb's *The Great Plains.* Corwin writes that Chicanos, among other things, ignore "the Spanish and Mexican retreat in desert regions before marauding Indians." This assessment by Corwin contains two basic contradictions: (1) McWilliams's thesis, notwithstanding Webb's statement, has not been disproved. I recommend that Corwin read Charles L. Kenner's *A History of New Mexican-Plains Indian Relations* (University of Oklahoma Press, 1969), which supports rather than detracts from McWilliams's frontier thesis. (2) While Corwin is vehement in his criticism of Chicano works, he significantly ignores the fact that Webb's works are often racist in their attitudes and assessments of Mexicans. Throughout his essay Corwin completely ignores Webb's *The Texas Rangers,* as he does the works of other ethnocentric historians, clearly underscoring his double standard in assessing Chicano and Anglo works. (Note: Webb himself admitted that his attitudes toward Mexicans were prejudicial and wished to have changed many of his conclusions. See the Walter Prescott Webb Papers at the University of Texas.)

Another example of Corwin's use of the double standard is his whitewash of the Mexican-American War: on pages 14–15, he completely ignores the works of Abiel Abbot Livermore, *The War with Mexico Reviewed* (American Peace Society, 1850), or Samuel E. Chamberlain, *My Confessions* (Harper and Brothers, 1956). Instead he dwells on such historians as Justin Smith who condemn Mexico as the guilty party. Corwin's failure to comment on Smith's chauvinism can only lead one to the conclusion that he approves of it. Moreover, he erroneously classifies Seymour V. Connor and Odie B. Faulk's *North America Divided: The Mexican War* as a revisionist work. This work is no more revisionist than that of Smith. It is a justification for United States aggression and is in the best tradition of nineteenth-century nationalistic histories. Furthermore, Corwin again ignores the sins of such Anglo historians as Faulk who are notorious for their championing the "winning of the West" philosophy, which is still prevalent among so many of the region's cowboy scholars.

In contrast Corwin is relentless in his criticism of the activist-Chicano scholar and of Chicano Studies in general. On Page 4, he labels "ethnic studies" as doctrinaire and chauvinistic. On page 35, he charges that Chicano Studies as well as history provides "catharsis for minority groups by giving ethnic studies representation in the academic curriculum . . ." and concludes that it fosters cultural nationalism and racial separatism. While Corwin does not offer any documentation, such as empirical studies of Chicano Studies programs, he attempts to substantiate his claims by citing a Spanish surnamed historian, Manuel A. Machado, Jr., who, Corwin says, deplores *"con salsa picante,* the trend toward polarization, demagoguery, and counterstereotyping that he feels only serves to abort a rational appreciation of the needs, functions, and place of ethnic history."

Again Corwin's contradictions are obvious: First, to my knowledge, Corwin has examined few if any Chicano Studies programs.* For instance, the Chicano Studies Department of California State University at Northridge has nineteen full-time professors and offers over eighty sections in Chicano Studies. Corwin has never visited that program, which, if he were an authority on Chicano Studies, he most certainly would have investigated. I can therefore only conclude that his assessments of Chicano Studies programs have been based on hearsay evidence or assumptions. Second, Manuel A. Machado, Jr., can hardly be called an expert on Chicano Studies. To my knowledge, he has never been associated with a

---

* I have been associated with Chicano Studies since the Fall of 1966 when I first taught a course on the History of the Mexican American at Mount Saint Mary's College. I have had ample opportunity to observe the formation and development of said programs.

Chicano Studies program and has done little or nothing to advance understanding between the Chicano and the Anglo-American. Quite the contrary, Machado has been the darling of the right wing and consistently been used to counter the so-called activists. We sincerely urge Corwin to examine primary sources, if at all possible, before he makes further comments on a subject he does not know anything about.

What Corwin is saying is that it is all right for Anglo-Americans to be chauvinistic but not for Chicanos. If the former do so, then it is scholarly, but if the latter advocate the cause of their group then it is polemical.

I would now like not only to document further Corwin's application of a double standard in assessing Chicano works, but also to expose how he not too skillfully attempted to impose his political ideology on this emerging field: he arbitrarily divides Chicanos into two camps—the La Raza school versus the "establishment school"; or the militant and moderates versus the conservatives. However, even in this endeavor, Corwin proves inept. For instance, Ralph Vigil and Manuel Servín, whom Corwin puts into the "establishment school," reject his presumptions, and Carlos Cortés, whom he also condemns to the "establishment school," is far from being a conservative or even a moderate.

In making his assessment of the literature, it is obvious that Corwin does not know the current trend in Chicano history. On pages 3–4, for instance, he asserts that Chicano scholars are dwelling on the themes of Aztlán and the Treaty of Guadalupe-Hidalgo. If Corwin would only make a survey of Chicano journals, he would learn that these themes have almost been entirely ignored in the past two years. Chicano historians are moving into such topics as labor and regional accounts. Moreover, much attention is being paid to new models, such as internal colonialism. Finally, Corwin does not even mention the current influence of Marxism, Frantz Fanon, psychohistory, or E. J. Hobsbawm on Chicano works, demonstrating again that much of his information on current scholarship is based on hearsay and supposition.

Corwin's use of cliches is frustrating: he totally writes off my *Occupied America,* not by attacking its theses or disproving that there has been exploitation, but by stating, on pages 7–8, that the thesis serves "to rationalize cultural separatism," that it is *"Mc-*

Williamismo carried from the sublime to the ridiculous," and that "it never leaves the reader in doubt as to the Brown Beret's view of southwestern history." However, Corwin does not offer one example to document his allegations nor does he attempt to define what the Brown Beret's version of history is.

As frustrating as Corwin's generalizations may be, what is alarming is his ignorance of a field which he has received a large grant from the National Endowment for the Humanities to study: "Mexican migration to the United States, 1900–1970." For instance, on page 19, he makes glaring errors of fact and omission. He writes that "After McWilliams there was no significant publication of historical interest on Mexican migration until economist Leo Grebler's monograph on twentieth-century *Mexican Immigration to the United States: The Record and Its Implications.*" Corwin completely ignores the master of arts thesis of Stella L. Carrillo, "Importancia Economica y Social de la Población Mexicana en Estados Unidos de Norteamerica" (M.A., México D.F.: Universidad Nacional Autonóma de México, 1963). Grebler drew heavily from Carrillo's work. In fact he was in constant communication with Carrillo who guided Grebler through Mexico in order that he could learn something about the people whom he had just received a half million dollars to study. Further, Corwin avoids mentioning Manuel H. Guerra and Y. Arturo Cabrera's critique of Grebler's Mexican-American Studies Project, a critique entitled *An Evaluation and Critique of "THE MEXICAN-AMERICAN STUDIES PROJECT,"* A Ford Foundation Grant Extended to the University of California at Los Angeles (Educational Council of the Mexican-American Political Association, 1966). The monograph raises questions which might add to Corwin's "assessment" of Chicano works as well as put him on notice as to what kind of pitfalls to avoid in the directorship of his own well-funded project.

It is evident that Corwin has used a double standard in judging Chicano and Anglo scholars. And, while I realize that subjective assessments cannot be totally divorced from any work, what I resent is attempts like that of Mr. Corwin to palm off opinions as scholarly and objective. If Corwin is a conservative, he should admit it instead of hiding behind such euphemisms as "scholarship." Furthermore, history is not the private fief of the militant, moderate, or right-winger. There must be an acceptance by all that Chicano history is not sectarian nor even in a separate category. The Chicano is a member of the Mexican family and is a product of its struggle within the context of Mexican and U.S. histories. In considering compromised works, such as that of Corwin, we must come to grips with the question of whether new models and perspectives will be allowed in evaluating the historical development of the Chicano in the United States, or whether the Corwins will be allowed to impose their dogma.

RODOLFO ACUÑA

California State University, Northridge

Once a Well-Kept Secret

Carey McWilliams

In this essay, the author of North from Mexico *explains how that seminal work came to be written.*

THE STORY OF HOW *North from Mexico* (Boston, 1949) came to be written has a relevance, if somewhat marginal, to the history of Mexican Americans as a minority. The book was projected, it should be noted, as part of a series—"The Peoples of America"— which was edited, in his lifetime, by my friend Louis Adamic. Adamic's great theme—his passion, one might say—was "the discovery of America." He had arrived at Ellis Island from Yugoslavia in 1913, alone, a youngster fifteen years of age who spoke not a word of English. To him the discovery of this country, more precisely the exploration of its cultural complexities and paradoxes, was an endlessly fascinating adventure. Louis was imaginative, highly intelligent, idealistic, a creature of immense enthusiasms. Almost everything about this country seemed to engage his attention and incite his curiosity. He brought a new vision to those aspects of American life about which he wrote. Not that he was uniformly enthusiastic about everything he discovered here; he saw many things that dismayed and disheartened him but few that did not interest him.

Naturally Adamic was interested in his own experience as an immigrant; it was indeed his first, and his most important, subject. Later he began to be interested in the experience of other immigrants and immigrant groups in general and to write about them. At an earlier date—say in the period of 1890 or thereabouts to 1914 —a large volume of writing, most of it extremely superficial, was devoted to a crude celebration of "the melting pot" concept and the glories of "Americanization." Some of it, of course, was stupid, morose, and biased, reflecting a deep fear of what was thought to be the

47

baneful and corrupting influence of immigrants on American society and its institutions. Most of this writing dated quickly so that when Adamic began to write about immigrants and immigrant subcultures in the 1930s, he brought a new and fresh interpretation to issues that had, over a period of years, receded in interest and become, so many Americans imagined, merely a phase of history. Adamic wrote as an immigrant, which most of the earlier commentators were not, and so brought to his experience a perception and sensitivity not to be found in their work.

He wrote, of course, long before the present-day modish emphasis on ethnics and ethnicity. But a brief quotation from *Grandsons*—one of his better books—will indicate that he was fully aware of "identity problems" and other ambiguities of the immigrant experience:

There were things in me (I was barely cognizant of them) which I did not want to see killed or harmed. I wanted to get into America and at her as a writer on my own terms. I didn't want the turbulent, superficial, temporary, non-essential America to get me altogether. She already had touched me too much. It was (as I now see it) my Carniolan peasant egoism, of course, that stood in the way of my thorough Americanization in the current sense; but not that alone. There were things in contemporary America that just naturally went against the grain. Violently so. I wanted nothing to do with them except fight them if I ever got a chance. . . . I was hysterical, but perhaps mainly because I was impatient with myself, bewitched and bewildered about America. I was twenty-eight, twenty-nine. Perhaps half my life was gone, possibly more, and where was I? I was spending most of my energy fighting the forces of jitteriness in contemporary America that had put their hooks into me personally, for unwittingly, ignorantly, I had exposed myself to them. They held me and I was uncomfortable; I felt like nothing at all, a shadow, no better than most people in America; but I would extricate myself from them. I was still partly an outsider. . . .[1]

On the eve of World War II, the Common Council of American Unity—an old-line immigrant-aid group based in New York—decided to launch a quarterly publication which would stress "unity and mutual understanding among peoples of diverse backgrounds in America." It was called *Common Ground,* and the first issue ap-

---

[1] *Grandsons* (New York, 1935), 80–81.

peared in August 1940. Adamic was the first editor and Margaret Anderson was his assistant. It survived for about a decade, but, after a year or so, Adamic stepped aside as editor. It published some excellent pieces about racial and ethnic minorities and about the problems of a multi-racial, multi-ethnic society. In a way "The Peoples of America" series, which Adamic began to edit for J. B. Lippincott Company in 1943, was an outgrowth not merely of his own writing but of his interest in *Common Ground*. Titles included "Americans from Holland" by Arnold Mulder, "Americans from Hungary" by Emil Lengyel, "Americans from Japan" by Bradford Smith, "Americans from Norway" by Leola Nelson Bergman, and "Americans from Ireland" by Shaemas O'Sheel. Louis talked to me at great length, off and on, about the series, and I suggested authors for some of the volumes, specifically, as I remember, D'Arcy McNickle for the book about Indians and J. Saunders Redding for the volume about Negroes. At some point in these talks, he asked me if I would do a volume about Mexican Americans and I agreed.

The point about this recital is quite simple. It would have been difficult to interest a general publisher in a book about Mexican Americans in the late 1940s. Mexican Americans were still not a "subject" of general interest and most publishers would have objected—stupidly—that too few of them spoke or read English. Even at that late date, Mexican Americans were regarded as a sociological and historical curiosity, somehow unrelated to, not an integral part of, the American scene. If, therefore, *North from Mexico* had not been projected as part of a series it would probably not have been published. On the other hand, the series was a sound publishing venture. It could be sold, as a series, to schools, colleges, and libraries, and, if some individual volumes sold better than others, that would help balance out the costs.

The reception the book received when it was first published in January 1949—and its subsequent history—also suggest the relative obscurity and marginality of Mexican Americans as a "subject" at that time. Books published as part of a series seldom receive the attention they might receive if published separately and *North from Mexico* was certainly no exception. It was almost totally ignored by the reviewing media. Of a handful of reviews, most were brief notes of the announcement variety. So the book, of course, got off to a bad start. Even so, it had a slow, steady sale in the first decade of publication. In 1960 or 1961 Lippincott informed me that the stock was nearly exhausted and that they did not intend to bring out another edition. So the rights reverted to me. In the meantime, I had moved to New York from California in 1951 to become an editor of *The Nation*. In 1961 the editors of Monthly Review Press (my friends, the late Leo Huberman and Paul Sweezy)—which then sublet office space from *The Nation*—said they would like to bring out an edition of the book with a new jacket. Rather to their surprise, and mine, this printing sold out rather quickly. It also resulted in a Spanish language edition which was issued in Mexico City (*Al Norte de México, el conflicto entre "anglos" e "hispanos,"* translated by Lys De Cardoza and published by Siglo XXI Editores, 1968). By 1968 the Monthly Review Press edition had been exhausted, but Greenwood Press decided to reissue the volume in a hardcover edition for which I wrote a brief introduction, and, when the book began to sell very well indeed, a paperback edition was published. Still later, the Educational Film Division of Greenwood produced a documentary film, *North from Mexico: Exploration and Heritage,* based on the book.

The Greenwood edition was well-timed. By 1968 the "position" of Mexican Americans had undergone a radical change. They had indeed become for the first time a "subject" of general national interest. The late Dr. George Sánchez of the University of Texas— whose friendship I cherished—once said of Mexican Americans that they were "an orphan group, the least known, the least sponsored, and the least vocal large minority group in the nation." Represenative Edward R. Roybal of California, himself of Mexican-American descent, confirmed this view by saying that "The Mexican population in the "Southwest . . . is little known on the East Coast and not much better understood in the Southwest itself." At about the same time a Mexican American was quoted in *Newsweek* as saying: "We're the best kept secret in America."

This was certainly the general view of Mexican Americans as late as 1949 when *North from Mexico* was published, and it prevailed well into the 1960s. But Mexican Americans have now come into the full view of the media; they have definitely arrived—witness feature stories about them in *The Wall Street Journal,* May 3, 1966; *Newsweek,* May 23, 1966; *Time,* April 28, 1967; and *U. S. News and*

World Report, June 6, 1966. More recently, of course, any number of books—studies, anthologies, source books—by and about Chicanos have appeared. Many factors, of course, might be cited to explain what appeared to be the "sudden" emergence of Mexican Americans into full view for the first time. The ferment occasioned by World War II, the political interest aroused by the *Viva Kennedy* clubs in 1960, the civil rights movement, the riots and disturbances of 1967, all played a part in the transforming process. But perhaps the chief factor was the growing social, economic, political, and educational maturity of the Mexican-American minority, a maturity reflected in the emergence of a sizable middle class and the appearance, for the first time, of significant numbers of Mexican Americans in colleges and universities, both as students and graduate students and (still more recently) as faculty; also, their appearance, in growing numbers, in the professions, in government service, and in politics. It is this rather swift emergence of the minority —although the process had been under way for a long time—which accounts for the fact that *North from Mexico* finally managed to attract, two decades after it was first published, a good-sized audience.

This same belated emergence of the Mexican-American minority no doubt accounts for the fact that I was asked to prepare *North from Mexico* for "The Peoples of America" series. Louis knew of my interest in Mexican Americans and that I had written about some aspects of their experience. It was natural that he should ask me to take the assignment. But it is also true that there were, at the time, only a few Mexican-American writers or persons of Spanish-speaking background who had written about Mexican Americans. Indeed, not a great deal had been written about them by anyone at that time.

I got interested in Mexican Americans in the early 1930s when I was living in southern California. My interest in them was part of a growing interest in the—to me—fascinating social history of California, more particularly the saga of migratory farm labor and the way in which one minority group after another had been recruited and used as farm workers. California, of course, is a splendid laboratory in which to study majority-minority relationships. Virtually all the various ethnic and racial strains in the American population are represented in this one state, including some which were not widely represented outside it, such as Japanese, Chinese, Filipinos, and Hindus. As a new and rapidly growing state, social relations have been kept more or less in a state of constant flux in California. Thus, certain patterns in majority-minority relationships are more visible there than elsewhere and can be seen with greater clarity.

In any case, I began to do magazine articles about some of California's minorities and their problems. And, of course, the more I wrote about these subjects the more interested I became in them. Also, as a member of the board of the American Civil Liberties Union in Los Angeles—for many years—I had occasion to become involved in some of the civil liberties issues affecting these groups. And because he knew of my interest in these matters Governor Culbert L. Olson asked me to head the Division of Immigration and Housing at the same time (January 1939) that he asked George Kidwell to become director of the Department of Industrial Relations of which it was a part. The Division had been the brainchild of Simon J. Lubin, a distinguished public citizen, and a man that I knew and greatly admired. At different times Carlton Parker, John Collier, and Justin Miller had served with the Division. A unique agency, the Division had a general responsibility for the condition of labor camps—mostly mining, lumber, railroad, and agricultural camps—and it also had been given power to inquire into the welfare of resident immigrants. Lubin had worked in a settlement house in New York and had earlier convinced Governor Hiram Johnson that, with the completion of the Panama Canal, a large flow of European immigration would be directed to the West Coast. It might have happened, too, if World War I had not intervened.

As head of the Division for four years—turbulent years in the history of farm labor, what with big strikes, the influx of 350,000 dustbowl migrants, and the tempestuous hearings of the LaFollette Committee—I had an unrivaled opportunity to investigate and observe farm labor conditions and, in the process, to become familiar with Filipinos, Mexican Americans, and other groups making up the huge pool of farm labor. When the Alien Registration Act was adopted, in part as a wartime measure, the Division worked closely, on my initiative, with the Immigration Service and Department of Labor to make sure that Mexican aliens knew about the law and how to comply with it. In the wake of this experience, and in part by way of summing it up, I wrote *Brothers under the Skin* (Boston, 1943), an overall view of the so-called "minorities problem," and, later, *Prejudice* (Boston, 1945), about the war-time experiences of Japanese Americans. Also, the research I did for *Factories in the Field* (Boston, 1939) and *Southern California Country: An Island on the Land* (New York, 1946) taught me something about Mexican Americans in California. *Ill Fares the Land* (Boston, 1942) deals with migratory farm labor nationally, so I had occasion, in writing it, to visit Mexican-American communities in the border states, in Michigan and Ohio, in Chicago, and elsewhere.

Also, as part of the ferment of the World War II period, the community of Los Angeles began to show a new interest in Mexican Americans, in part because of the implications of the Good Neighbor Policy and also because new stirrings of unrest began to take place in the Mexican-American settlements. The Sleepy Lagoon murder case of 1942—I served as chairman of the Sleepy Lagoon Defense Committee which ultimately secured the acquittal of the defendants—aroused a great deal of interest and uneasiness. Antagonisms began to mount when a representative of the sheriff's office made some excessively silly remarks about Mexican Americans. In an effort to "cool it," the Los Angeles County Grand Jury decided to hold hearings on some of the problems of Mexican Americans. I testified, at some length, at these hearings on October 2, 1942. The larger community was certainly placed on notice that serious trouble was to be anticipated, but no remedial measures were taken. And so, in June 1943, the so-called Zoot Suit Riots occurred. In the aftermath of the riots, Attorney General Robert W. Kenny asked me to prepare a report which could be used—and was used—as a draft report for the committee of inquiry named by Governor Earl Warren. Actually I had a hand in inducing Kenny to induce Warren to name the committee.

The foregoing recital is also by way of preface to making a point. Anyone caught up as I was in the social ferment of the 1930s and in such a yeasty state as California; anyone, who had the experiences with particular racial and ethnic minorities that I had, could not avoid being tagged, now and then, as a "spokesman" for this group or that or, more generally, as a "spokesman" for minorities. The fact is that I never fancied myself in any such role and whenever an appropriate occasion arose, I went out of my way to reject it. A

basic aspect of my thinking about minorities is that they must—
and they always do eventually—develop their own spokesmen before the essence of their experiences can properly be communicated
to others. My interest in minorities and in majority-minority relationships is an intellectual interest; I have always found the subject
most intriguing. It forms, in my view, a central aspect of the problem of evolving a truly democratic society. What my writings about
minorities represent is not an attempt to "speak for" this group or
that but to alleviate my ignorance; I have been, in a word, conducting my education in public, in print. Nothing that I learned in
college or university provided a usable background. If youngsters
today complain about the lack of relevance in their education, they
should have attended the courses I took in economics, sociology, and
politics in the 1920s. The sociology texts, insofar as they touched on
race relations, were inadequate and misleading. "Social distance"
was a favorite concept. Graduate students were sent out, armed with
questionnaires, in an effort to measure the "social distance" between
groups as reflected in attitudes. "Prejudice" was discussed as though
it were somehow an inescapable aspect of "differences" in language,
skin color, or characteristics that managed to be described as though
they were genetic. If my educational background on majority-
minority relationship was meager-to-barren, my family background
also offered little assistance. I spent my boyhood on a cattle ranch
and small town in northwestern Colorado where "contacts" with
persons of different racial and ethnic background were severely
limited. The word "Jew," for example, had largely biblical or
literary connotations for me until I was a freshman in college. In
brief, I had to learn about majority-minority relations by investigating these relations at first hand and as an outgrowth of my interest in the subject.

*   *   *

Now perhaps we may be on the verge of overcoming the preconditions for the evolution of the kind of democracy in which we pur-
port to believe. For example, the institution of slavery had to be
toppled and the 13th, 14th, and 15th amendments adopted, as a
basic precondition. No sooner had this happened, however, than
rapid industrial expansion attracted millions of immigrants and

each of these groups had in turn to overcome various barriers and discriminations before they could get a real foothold in the society. The long, bloody struggle to establish the right of working people to form unions which could bargain for their members was really a part of this same struggle. At a later date, immigrants were subjected not merely to discrimination and frontal assaults of one kind or another but also to social pressures—which were part of the "Americanization" program—to "assimilate." Some aspects of this program were sensible enough but it was flawed by an obsessive insistence that minorities must assimilate right now, this instant, on terms dictated by the majority. Only now are some of these groups beginning to acquire a status and to assert a cultural identity, and political position, which can protect them against manipulation by dominant groups. Nowadays, of course, the new emphasis on ethnicity and ethnic identity has managed to offset some of the pressures associated with what might be called forced assimilation. Indeed, the new emphasis may be creating some new problems; a common culture, which can be shared by all, is still a necessary precondition for the evolution of a truly democratic society.

Other preconditions are in process of being achieved. With assistance from others, Indians have begun to attain a new maturity, educational, economic, and political—a necessary precondition to their ability to offset old disabilities and injustices. Blacks had to achieve, through a new emphasis on black power and group pride, a measure of self-organization, self-determination, and self-direction before a real beginning could be made to reverse the blighting consequences of chattel slavery. Mexican Americans had to start down the path on which they are now moving before we could expect anything like a "greening" of America. Mexican Americans were not thought of as "immigrants" nor did they think of themselves as such. They did not cross an ocean; they simply moved north from Mexico. They have not been handicapped by a heritage of chattel slavery but their experience has been darkened by memories of the Mexican-American War and the ill-will and mutual distrust it engendered. What Indians, blacks, and Mexican Americans have been doing to free themselves from subordinate status, most European immigrant groups have done in times past. The parallels are not exact—there are important differences—but they are similar. What currently bothers some Americans as an overemphasis on group solidarity, even a kind of chauvinism-in-reverse, is, I feel, a passing phase, part of a process. None of this is to imply that all the necessary preconditions have been established for the evolution of a democratic society; far from it. But headway is being made and perhaps somewhat faster than we imagine. We will never achieve such a society until the structure of concentrated economic, social, and political power, and the inequalities it fosters, has itself been democratized. But the emergence of minorities, all of them into the mainstream of American life, and their full participation in its culture and politics, is itself a precondition for the achievement of this larger goal.

Carlos Eduardo Castañeda, Mexican-American Historian: The Formative Years, 1896-1927

Félix D. Almaráz, Jr.

The author is a member of the history department in the University of Texas, San Antonio.

IN THE ANNALS of southwestern historiography, the name of Carlos Eduardo Castañeda stands majestically as a hallmark of sound scholarship and inspirational teaching. No Mexican-American historian in this century has approximated his solid publishing record of twelve books and seventy-eight articles. Likewise, no educator of Mexican descent in the United States has received as many honors and distinctions as were conferred on Don Carlos in his lifetime. From the hierarchy of the Catholic Church, Castañeda received knighthood in the Order of the Holy Sepulchre of Jerusalem; from the Academy of American Franciscan History, the Serra Award of the Americas; and from Spain, knighthood in the Order of Isabela the Catholic. Moreover, he was recognized as a true Pan American- ist with membership in the Texas Philosophical Society, the His- panic Society of America, the Academia de Historia de Guatemala, and the Centro de Estudios de Argentina.

Physically Castañeda was of medium stature, but intellectually,

Reaserch for this article was made possible by a grant from the National Endow- ment for the Humanities.

as his students have testified, he was a giant. Of his prodigious bibliography, two titles have clearly withstood the test of time: *The Mexican Side of the Texan Revolution* and the seven-volume *Our Catholic Heritage in Texas, 1519–1936*. For Castañeda, however, the work of which he was proudest was his doctoral dissertation, an annotated translation of Fray Juan Agustín Morfi's long-lost *History of Texas,* published in a beautiful two-part edition by the Quivira Society of New Mexico.[1] In the world of academia, Castañeda led a quiet and productive life, continually striving to perfect his style and technique as a Texas historian of first rank. Yet very few people today are aware of the formative years when Don Carlos began the odyssey that led to the University of Texas at Austin.

Carlos Eduardo, the seventh child of Timoteo and Elisa Andrea Castañeda, was born on November 11, 1896, in the border town of Ciudad Camargo, Tamaulipas. His father, a Yucatecan who had been educated in San Antonio, Texas, was a progressive-minded civic leader in Camargo during the Porfirio Díaz administration. In 1902 ,the elder Castañeda ran unsuccessfully for the governorship of Tamaulipas, after which he turned to teaching. Convinced that the Díaz regime was on the brink of collapse, Timoteo Castañeda took his family with him to Matamoros, where he became an instructor at the Colegio de San Juan.[2] Shortly thereafter, in 1906, part of the Castañeda family, Carlos included, moved across the Rio Grande to Brownsville, while the other members remained in Mexico.

Although Carlos had begun his education in Matamoros, he had to repeat two primary grades when he enrolled in the Brownsville schools because he was literate only in Spanish. To compensate for this setback, he took his parents' advice and attended summer sessions until he mastered the English language. Then, by skipping

1 Juan Agustín Morfi, *History of Texas, 1673–1779,* translated and edited by Carlos E. Castañeda (2 vols., Albuquerque, New Mex., 1935). See also Félix D. Almaráz, Jr., "Profile of a Reformer: Carlos E. Castañeda—Educator, Historian, Author" (unpublished address, Alpha Chi Lecture No. 1, Pan American University, Edinburg, Texas, May 4, 1970).

2 Taped interview with Josephine Castañeda, Brownsville, Texas, Dec. 15, 1970 (tape and transcript in the archives of the University of Texas, San Antonio); Elsie Upton, "A Knight of Goodwill," *St. Joseph Magazine,* XLIV (June 1943), 12, in Casteñeda biographical file, Texas Collection, University of Texas Library, Austin.

two grades, he advanced to a class of his own age group. In 1909, before he entered high school, his parents died within a few months of one another, first his father and then his mother. The impact of parental loss instilled in him a deep sense of responsibility toward his unmarried sisters which remained with him throughout his adult life. "He was a very familial boy," his youngest sister, Josephine, recalls. "I mean, he had three older sisters and one younger sister, and he was the only boy [left at home]. So he was very devoted to his family. And he assumed the responsibility right away."[3] By the age of twelve he had a job in a store selling groceries and clothes. "He made three dollars a week," Josephine remembers, "and he would bring those three dollars worth of groceries home, all his pay. And he kept working at this place until he learned how to type and then he was in the buying and manager of the place. While he was going to school he did that, just after school."

Castañeda's high school years were thus filled with curricular and extracurricular activities. Like most youngsters, he enjoyed swimming, horseback riding, and hunting, but he also reflected the earlier influence of his parents and his own love of books by insisting that "his school work always came first."[4] Through diligent application to his studies at Brownsville High School, he graduated in 1916 as valedictorian of his class. In fact, he was the only Mexican American in the group that received diplomas at Hinkley Hall on May 23.[5]

Don Carlos's achievements won for him a scholarship to the University of Texas, but he did not attend classes in the fall semester because of financial difficulties, namely unpaid taxes on the family home. To raise money to pay the delinquent assessments and to meet expenses at the university, he taught at an ungraded county school at Las Palmas, near Brownsville.[6] In 1917, he arrived in Aus-

---

[3] Castañeda's other sisters were María, Andrea Lisa, and Elisa Leonila. Castañeda assumed a life-long financial responsibility for all his sisters except one who married. Interview with Josephine Castañeda.

[4] *Ibid.*

[5] Program, Baccalaureate Services, May 21, 1916, and Commencement Program, May 23, 1916, in the Carlos E. Castañeda Papers (in the possession of Mrs. Carlos E. Castañeda, 301 West 37th Street, Austin, Texas).

[6] M. C. Gonzáles, "Honoring Dr. C. E. Castañeda," *Lulac News*, I (July 1932), 3 (in the possession of Josephine Castañeda, Brownsville, Texas); Upton, "Knight of Goodwill," 12; Tom Bowman Brewer, "A History of the Department of History of the University of Texas, 1883–1951" (M. A. thesis, University of Texas, 1957), 116.

tin with about sixty dollars and a firm determination to get a degree in engineering. The chaplain of the Newman Club, Father John Elliott Ross, aware of Castañeda's financial difficulties, invited him to live rent free in the "tiny garrett above St. Austin's chapel." Years later, Castañeda the historian reminisced about his brief collision with engineering and about the influence on his life of Eugene C. Barker, the crusty chairman of the history department at the University of Texas.

I had decided to be an engineer for no better reason than I had done well in mathematics in high school. But Father Ross and Dr. Eugene C. Barker . . . helped me to find my real life work. Doctor Barker gave me a job copying the letters of Stephen F. Austin, thus giving me my first real insight into the field of history. My great ambition at that time was to write as well as Doctor Barker.[7]

Castañeda's introduction to Barker left him with a life-long fascination with history. "My work as a typist and general assistant to Dr. Barker," he later recalled, "was of inestimable value. . . . I learned much that is not taught in classrooms about honest scholarship and the painstaking accuracy required of the historian; I learned how to handle manuscripts and I experienced the sheer joy of reconstructing the past from stray scraps, notes, letters, documents, those bits of men's minds and hearts that are traced in black and white on paper made frail by age. Handling old manuscripts as I did in my initiation to history was as printer's ink [is] to the printer, as the smell of powder [is] to the soldier. It was fascinating and exciting; it got under my skin and into my blood."[8]

In the spring of 1918, Castañeda's education was interrupted when he enlisted in the United States Army. For the duration of World War I he served as a machine gun instructor at Camp Mabry, in northwestern Austin. In an effort to get assigned to Europe, he requested a transfer to the navy or to heavy artillery where officers with a background in engineering were needed, but the war ended before a decision on his transfer could be rendered.[9] Out of uniform, Castañeda returned to the University of Texas, but within a

---

7 Upton, "Knight of Goodwill," 12.
8 Carlos E. Castañeda, "Why I Chose History," *The Americas,* VIII (1952), 477.
9 Upton, "Knight of Goodwill," 12.

semester, because of insufficient funds, he left Austin and migrated
to Tampico where he found employment in the engineering department of the Mexican Gulf Oil Company. For about a year Don
Carlos gained practical experience in railroad engineering, pipe
line surveys, land surveying, construction work, and other aspects
of civil engineering. Interesting and challenging as he undoubtedly considered the job in Mexico, he yearned to return to the university and to obtain a degree in history. In a letter to Eugene C.
Barker, Castañeda unfolded his plans to the teacher who had become his mentor.

As time draws near for the new school year, I am writing to tell you
that I have not given up the idea of coming back and finishing as I intended when I first set out for Mexico. I have often intended writing
you, but I assure you [that] the life of an engineer in the oil fields is far
from being Ideal [sic] and it offers very few opportunities for writing to
anyone. The question of getting mail out in the fields is almost a hope-
less one, and when you take into consideration the fact that I have been
most of the time absolutely out in the woods away even from the out-of-
town camps, you will understand how it is that I did not write you before.

How are things in Austin? I hope you took a vacation this summer,
and that you are well. Personally I believe that my change of work has
done me good, and I feel that I can take up my school work with a little
more enthusiasm, and a broad[er] attitude than last fall. Have you any
more typewriting work this year? Is there any opportunity of getting an
assistan[t]ship in the History Department? If there is, please keep me in
mind. . . .[10]

Though an assistantship in the history department was unavail-
able, Castañeda found other means of support when he returned to
the University of Texas in the fall of 1920. He won the first George
Tarleton scholarship. This money, combined with funds provided
by an anonymous Catholic friend of higher education, enabled him
to complete the program in history without going into debt. In
1921, Don Carlos earned a Phi Beta Kappa key and a Bachelor of
Arts degree.[11]

After graduation, Castañeda, even with Barker's help, was unable

10 Castañeda to Eugene C. Barker., Aug. 10, 1920, Eugene C. Barker Papers, 1918–
1920, Eugene C. Barker Texas History Center, University of Texas Library, Austin.
11 Upton, "Knight of Goodwill," 12.

to find what he wanted most—a college teaching position. He finally took a job at a high school in Beaumont, Texas. Like many other young teachers—and older ones, for that matter—his reaction to his new assignment was mixed. "School teaching . . . ," he confided to Barker about six weeks after the opening of the 1921–1922 academic year, "is not such an easy job as I expected. However, I am not displeased with the work, but rather enjoy it. I would be entirely happy if it were not for a few who seem to think their whole aim in life is to make the teacher's life miserable. I am getting used to high school ways again. I had a hard time at first, for I expected the students to behave somewhat as University men. I do not hold that delusion anymore."[12]

Despite the heavy obligations imposed by a first-year teaching schedule, Castañeda took other jobs that helped him earn enough to support his sisters in Brownsville. He taught a Spanish class at the local Y. M. C. A. and another in the high school's extended day program. Altogether he taught four nights a week in addition to his regular day school assignments. Though his commitments were heavy, he began casting plans for graduate work. "When the time for the opening of school came, I mean the University," he confessed to Barker in October 1921, "I felt a little homesick. I wanted to go back pretty bad. My intention has been to do some work on my thesis, but up to the present I have been too busy getting my teaching work started to think very much of anything else. I intend to begin doing some reading before this month is over. Dr. [Charles Wilson] Hackett . . . had promised to send me the books I need from time to time and I am going to avail myself of the opportunity."[13]

Barker encouraged his young friend, but he also warned him not to overextend himself. "I see that you are up to your old trick of doing about twice as much work as the ordinary mortal is willing to tackle," he wrote Castañeda. "Don't overdue [sic] it." But, he added, "I see no reason why you should not be able to get forward with some reading on your thesis, though it is very likely that most of your work in [primary] sources will have to be done here on the spot. I have no doubt that Hackett will send you such books as you

---

12 Castañeda to Barker, Oct. 15, 1921, Barker Papers.
13 *Ibid.*

write for if it is possible to let them leave the Library." Then he counseled Castañeda about a personal problem. "Don't forget to practice my advice about your pronunciation. Slow down your speech and speak more distinct. It will increase your efficiency not merely in the high school but in anything that you later decide to do."[14]

For Castañeda to reduce the pace of his speech pattern or his schedule of activities was like trying to change the direction of a Texas "Norther." Toward the end of 1921 he accepted additional responsibilities. "I do not know what you are going to think about it," he told Barker, "but I have just decided to try to do one more thing in addition to the others and that is to get married. Perhaps this will not be a very great surprise, for I have been contemplating this step for some time and at last I have made up my mind to do it."[15]

Very likely because of the upcoming wedding, Castañeda cut down on his work schedule, but the slow down proved to be only temporary. His desire to become an historian was increasing, and to an impatient historian-in-the-making research and writing were inseparable tasks on which he was anxious to begin work. Indeed, somehow he had already found time to engage in scholarly activity. "Soon after I arrived here [in Beaumont, Texas]," he wrote Barker in November 1921, "I finished a short article on the missions of Texas, which Father Ross thought good enough to send to the Missionary Magazine, and I received a check for it yesterday. I will send you a copy of it; that you may read it if you have the time."[16]

Much to Castañeda's disappointment Barker was unable to attend his wedding at San Fernando Cathedral in San Antonio, on December 27, 1921, when Don Carlos married Elisa Ríos, a refugee whose family had fled from Mexico to Brownsville and later to the Alamo city. Since Castañeda's parents had been married at the cathedral, the selection of San Fernando was an observance of tradition. The ceremony, officiated by Father Ross of the Newman Club, was the "consumation of a four-year romance."[17] Following the wedding, the Castañedas set up housekeeping at 1493 Hazel

14 Barker to Castañeda, Oct. 19, 1921, *ibid.*
15 Castañeda to Barker, Nov. 16, 1921, *ibid.*
16 *Ibid.*
17 Upton, "Knight of Goodwill," 12–13.

Street in Beaumont. The responsibility of a new family, combined with Carlos's obligation to provide for the welfare of his sisters in Brownsville, prompted the young husband to look about for additional sources of income. But his duties notwithstanding, he continued to make plans to begin graduate studies at the University of Texas in the summer of 1922. The prospects of needed summer employment on the campus looked bleak, however. "There will be nothing that we can do for you in the History Department this next summer," Barker told him. "All our funds are used up and there seems little likelihood that we can get any additional money. Of course it is always possible that a little typewriting may turn up, but one makes little at that sort of thing. It is a little late for you to apply for anything in Spanish, but there is always a possibility that an unexpected vacancy may occur, so that it can do no harm whatever for you to write to Miss [Lilia M.] Casis [of the Spanish Department] about something."[18] On the personal side, Barker inquired:

I wonder if you have gotten rid of some of your rapid enunciation and have learned to separate words. You know I have insisted many times that you must slow down your speech if you were ever to make a successful teacher. I hope that your experience in the high school has helped you to remedy that trouble. I suppose that it is a simpton [sic] of your nervous disposition, aggravated by the tremendous pressure under which you have always worked. Now that you have become a settled married man, I hope that you will not live at such high speed.[19]

Castañeda was disappointed with Barker's reply about the lack of job openings at the University, but he was not discouraged. He continued to look for new opportunities and, in the spring of 1922, he was buoyed by the possibility of studying at the University of Mexico and doing research in the Mexican archives on a thesis project. He turned to Barker for advice.

I have just heard that the Mexican Government is offering a free trip to all teachers that desire to take up some work in the University of Mexico this summer. It pays the transportation expenses from the border to the capital as well as the return trip to the border. I believe that this

18 Barker to Castañeda, March 18, 1922, Barker Papers.
19 *Ibid.*

is a very good opportunity for me to visit Mexico city [sic] but the question is can I do any work there that will count towards my M. A.? I have most of my credit work done with the exception of a third of a course in Spanish and a course in History. If I were decided on the subject of my thesis I might be able to look up some material while I am in Mexico, but I am not.

What do you think about the matter? Would it be worth my while to go? Or would it be better that I stay in Austin this summer and try to do as much as I can there?[20]

Barker urged Castañeda to forget about the Mexican venture and to devote the summer to completing his course work at the University of Texas. To help out the financially embarrassed young man, he turned his house over to the Castañedas who lived in it rent free during the summer term.[21] When it came time to select a thesis topic, Barker suggested that Carlos catalog and analyze the Spanish and Mexican documents in the county courthouse in San Antonio. If Castañeda could secure a teaching position in the city school district, he could examine the archival holdings during his off-duty hours. Castañeda once more took his mentor's advice. He moved to San Antonio in August 1922, secured a teaching job, and began working in the local archives. Inadequate income continued to be a serious problem, however. Although the inner-city school administrators of San Antonio had credited his record with three years of teaching experience in Austin and Beaumont, he was given an annual salary of only $1,410, and assigned as a teacher of Spanish to George W. Brackenridge High School.[22] Despite the credit given him for his earlier experience, his salary was less than what he had made in Beaumont. To make up for the difference, he organized a special Spanish class for teachers which he taught twice a week in the evenings.

But Castañeda did not permit his financial difficulties to sidetrack his research. Barker also continued to offer words of encouragement, and, in October 1922, he dispatched a copy of Owen Coy's *Guide to the County Archives of California* for Don Carlos to consult in

---

20 Castañeda to Barker, April 24, 1922, *ibid.*

21 Interview with Mrs. Carlos Castañeda, May 29, 1972.

22 Teachers Salary and Service Records, Directory of San Antonio City Schools for Year Ending May 31, 1923, in Administrative Offices, San Antonio Independent School District, San Antonio, Texas.

drafting an outline of the Bexar County documents. Specifically Barker counseled:

I should say that your study should begin with a brief introductory history of Bexar County. This should include an account of (1) the position of San Antonio in Spanish and Mexican Texas, and (2) the position of San Antonio in Anglo-American Texas. This should be divided into a number of divisions. For example, San Antonio and Bexar County to 1846—A Frontier Community; and the period since Annexation, describing among other things the history of the political boundaries of the County; and a discussion of the racial elements and of their contributions and influences in the history of the section. You can get a good deal of your narrative on the county boundaries from Gammel's Laws of Texas (use the index).[23]

Barker expected a scholary as well as a practical study, one which would be a useful tool in southwestern historiography. The instructions to Castañeda became more precise.

Coming now to the archives, your thesis should give the classifications and survey all the county archives in the model found in this book; but you should, I think, combine with your survey a fuller description of the various classes of material than is given in the [California] book.

I think you should examine and describe the Spanish records pretty fully, paying particular attention to early deeds, wills, and mortgages. Look inside the various volumes and give an indication of the important historical features of the different records. Do the same, of course, for the County and District Court Records. I think you will find the records of the District Court kept separate from those of the County Clerk.

State the condition of the records—whether they are bound and in good order and whether or not they are indexed.

These are merely suggestions. Your own study will indicate to you, no doubt, any additional points to be covered. Use your historical judgment and get the stuff that is worthwhile for a historian to know.[24]

With these guidelines, Castañeda meticulously classified the county documents throughout the remainder of the 1922–1923 school year. The routine of academic life soon changed with the birth of a daughter, Gloria. Now there was one more mouth to feed. At the end of the spring semester, with the thesis still in an un-

23 Barker to Castañeda, Oct. 23, 1922, Barker Papers.
24 Ibid.

completed stage, Castañeda applied for an associate professorship in the Spanish department of William and Mary College in Williamsburg, Virginia. He asked Barker for a recommendation and reported that "Schools closed last Friday and I am going to start to work systematically on my thesis within the next day or two. I will let you know how I am getting along."[25]

The double strain of teaching and classifying the county records convinced Don Carlos to take a short vacation in Mexico. Characteristically, however, he devoted little time to leisure. Instead, he studied the public school system of several states as well as that of the federal district. He even interviewed the superintendents of Nuevo León, Coahuila, San Luis Potosí, and Querétaro, all of whom provided him with "a great number of bulletins and other facts concerning the general school system in those states." In Mexico City he conferred with the Minister of Public Instruction, José Vasconcelos, from whom he obtained "additional information" upon which to base a series of articles on Mexican education.[26] The history of Spanish Texas, however, remained his foremost concern. He informed Barker that while in Querétaro he had "made a special effort to locate some of the records of the famous Querétaro college of the Franciscans. I was not quite successful, but I located a man who I think will be able to give me a great deal of information as to what became of the library of the college of the Holy Cross [Nuestra Señora de la Santa Cruz de Querétaro]. I am sure that there ought to be some interesting documents there with regard to the Missions of Texas, since the missionaries started from there."[27] He then made a firm promise to Barker. "I intend to put all my time both day and night on my thesis from now on." His plan was to obtain his M. A. in time for the August, 1923, commencement.

Striving hard to meet the deadline that he had imposed on himself, Don Carlos, in early August 1923, sent a lengthy report to Barker describing technical problems that had to be resolved in order to complete the county records project. "I am almost sick with worry about my thesis," he wrote. "I have been working steadily every day . . . and I am not anywhere near through yet. I have over

---

25 Castañeda to Barker, May 28, 1923, *ibid.*
26 Castañeda to Barker, July 19, 1923, *ibid.*
27 *Ibid.*

1300 cards made out already, and there must be at least 400 more manuscripts to be gone over. I have finished taking notes on all the official papers. . . . I have also finished all the Mission papers . . . and have started and done about 150 pieces of the miscellaneous stuff. . . . I have been thinking that when I get all the cards copied they are going to make quite a bulky thesis for I do not think that I can copy more than ten cards to a page and at that rate there will be about 150 pages of index data alone. . . ."[28] Two days later Castañeda mailed another disappointing report.

When troubles come they come not [as] single spies, as Hamlet says, for I was sick all day yesterday. I had some kind of trouble with my stomach, and it pained me considerably, so I had to lay off all day. The day before they closed the County Clerk's office on account of the funeral ceremonies of President Harding, so you see I have been hadnicapped [sic] right and left. I hope I have no more trouble. Please send me a copy of a thesis to use as a model for the title page, and other mechanical details.[29]

Barker did more than help with technical details. Both he and Professor Charles William Ramsdell sent words of encouragement to the distressed young man, and they also agreed that he should limit his thesis to an analysis of the Spanish documents in the San Antonio archives. Even the modified project was formidable, but Castañeda managed to finish his thesis—349 pages of text—in time to be graduated at the end of the 1923 summer session.[30] Fourteen years later, the Yanaguana Society published the thesis, thus helping to fulfill Barker's prophecy about the ultimate usefulness of the study.[31] In the meantime, after graduation, the road to Virginia beckoned. The College of William and Mary had offered Carlos a job.

Castañeda's years at William and Mary were difficult as well as fruitful. For nearly a year his wife was seriously ill. During the months that she was confined to a hospital he often walked a mile and a half into the country to see their daughter who had to be

---

[28] Castañeda to Barker, Aug. 10, 1923, *ibid.*

[29] Castañeda to Barker, Aug. 12, 1923, *ibid.*

[30] Carlos E. Castañeda, "A Report on the Spanish Archives in San Antonio, Texas" (M. A. thesis, University of Texas, 1923).

[31] Castañeda, *A Report on the Spanish Archives in San Antonio, Texas* (San Antonio, 1937).

placed in the care of a babysitter.[32] Financial problems also continued to plague the family. "Although I have been diligently scouting for private tutoring with a view to getting some extra spending money," he lamented to Barker, "I find that there is none here. Of course, translations are out of the question in this small town, and in Norfolk, where I go once a week on extension work, I have not succeeded in finding anything either. I have become reconciled to the facts, and I am going to use my spare time on some other pursuits."[33] Barker commiserated with his young friend, and suggested that he might devote his spare time to translating an important primary source for Texas history, the statistical report prepared in 1835 by Juan Nepomuceno Almonte.

Don Carlos responded enthusiastically to Barker's suggestion. By early 1924 he had located a copy of the Almonte report in the Library of Congress, which agreed to loan him the volume through interlibrary services. In the meantime, however, Mrs. Castañeda had become so ill that she had to be hospitalized. In mid-February, Castañeda notified Barker that Doña Elisa's sickness had delayed the translation of the Almonte report and that the congressional library had recalled the book. All the same, he assured the Texas professor, "I am going to ask for it again sometime next month in order to finish the rest of it. I have almost half of it translated now."[34]

Working on a Texas topic, especially during Mrs. Castañeda's convalescence, no doubt contributed to Don Carlos's growing homesickness. Earlier he had asked Barker to inquire into the possibility of a summer school position in Texas, but remembering past disappointments he accepted William and Mary's first offer to teach both summer terms. Up to this juncture in Castañeda's life, the associate professorship at William and Mary had been the highlight in his professional career, but his thoughts constantly returned to Texas. For a short time, Ohio State University attracted him, but nothing substantial materialized at that institution.[35] Castañeda was never serious about Ohio, except by way of curious inquiry. His roots were in Texas, and he longed to return there at the first opportunity. To do so, of course, necessitated finding a teaching position. Again, in April 1924, he sought Barker's counsel:

---

32 Upton, "Knight of Goodwill," 13.
33 Castañeda to Barker, Oct. 29, 1923, Barker Papers.
34 Castañeda to Barker, Feb. 15, 1924, *ibid.*
35 *Ibid.*

My plans [he wrote] are to stay here [in Virginia] this summer and all of next year, but I sincerely hope to be able to go back to some school in Texas after that. For as you know my sisters are anxious for me to be nearer home [Brownsville]. It is a little too early of course to try looking around for a place down there but since I am so anxious to secure something there I would like to know what you could suggest as to how to go about securing a position either in a college or normal school, whether in History or Spanish. The truth of the matter is that I have made up my mind to work in Texas or some place nearby . . . to be able to help my sisters more directly. They write me often and they are always lamenting the fact that I am so far away. . . . I thought for a while I would apply for a position in all of the normal schools and universities in the state in hopes I would secure at least one favorable reply, but I wonder if that would be advisable or the best method to pursue. . . .[36]

Candid as Castañeda's plea seemed, perhaps it was the declaration in the closing paragraphs of the letter that especially caught Barker's attention. "I am still hoping," he wrote, "to go on for my Doctors Degree. Just where I will do my graduate work I have not decided yet, but I know that I must do it in the next two or three years." He reminded Barker that his study of the Mexican educational system had resulted in some nice dividends. "I have been writing a number of articles and have succeeded in having five published so far. There is not much money in it, but it is good advertisement; so I am keeping it up."

Barker's response to Castañeda was forthright and sympathetic. "I do not believe it would be a good idea to fire a broad side at all of the Texas colleges," he cautioned, "but with the opening of the fall term it would be well to make some inquiries of a selected few. . . ." Barker was even more encouraging about Castañeda's desire to pursue a graduate program in history. "I still have some hope that we may be able to place you in history and enable you to go on with your Doctor's degree in History. I am glad to hear that you have been writing and finding a medium of publication for your articles. Keep it up and keep copies of your articles to file with applications in the future."[37]

Since a teaching appointment or doctoral program in Texas was very much in the realm of speculation, Castañeda devoted the sum-

---

36 Castañeda to Barker, April 21, 1924, *ibid.*
37 Barker to Castañeda, May 10, 1924, *ibid.*

mer months of 1924 to his work at William and Mary while his family vacationed in San Antonio. In September misfortune struck again in the form of more illness and financial setbacks. "Mrs. Castañeda caught a very bad cold in Texas and developed a case of bronchitis," he wrote to Barker. "I had to go as far as New Orleans for her because she was unable to travel by herself. The doctors advise absolute rest for her so she is pratically an invalid. Her illness has thrown me completely out of balance financially and I am hard up. I wonder whether there is any translation or copying of something I could do for you up here to help myself along? . . . Writing articles does not pay financially. I wrote a number of things last winter and had them all published but the material returns were very little."[38] As much as much as Barker wanted to help Castañeda in this critical period, the most he could do was to advise him to hold on in Virginia until something definite turned up in Texas.

Better news for Carlos came from the William and Mary administration which, in 1925, named him to the directorship of a program called "Summer School in Mexico." The appointment raised Castañeda's spirits, not only because it gave him an opportunity to teach history, but also because it promised to provide him with additional funds. "I am working very hard to make the proposed Summer School in Mexico a success," he happily informed Barker. "I have secured official recognition by the University of Mexico and have been appointed to their regular faculty for the summer. I am going to teach a course in Latin American History in English and also a course in the Governments of Spanish America. I am reviewing my history and government to get ready. If the thing is a success and I manage to get a good crowd of students to go with me, I will make a little money besides the advertisement which I will get. If the plan fails it will not be for lack of advertisement for I am doing all I can to keep it before the public."[39]

Additional good news was the publication of the Almonte report. Castañeda had completed the translation and, in January 1925, he published the report in the *Southwestern Historical Quarterly*.[40]

---

38 Castañeda to Barker, Sept. 10, 1924, *ibid.*

39 Castañeda to Barker, Feb. 10, 1925, *ibid.*

40 Carlos E. Castañeda (trans.), "Statistical Report on Texas by Juan N. Almonte, 1935," *Southwestern Historical Quarterly*, XXVIII (Jan. 1925), 177–222.

The success of this venture prompted his mentor, Barker, to suggest an idea which eventually resulted in *The Mexican Side of the Texan Revolution*. "There are several other little books of the period of Almonte's report," wrote Barker, "which, I think, would be well worth translating. I am wondering, however, about the feasibility of a more ambitious project—namely, a translation of [Vicente] Filisola. This . . . is a two volume history of the Texas Revolution."[41]

Castañeda responded enthusiastically to the proposal, though for the time being the Mexican summer school program required his full attention. He was able to persuade "a good crowd of students" to go with him, thus assuring the success of the program and winning for himself an appointment as director of a similar project the following year.[42] Although the trips to Mexico were brief, they brought Castañeda through Texas where he reestablished his contacts in Austin. Finally, in 1927, unable to endure another season away from close friends and relatives, Castañeda, with the help of Barker, returned to the University of Texas as librarian of the Latin American collection. The long odyssey was over, for Castañeda had come home to stay.

Though Castañeda's struggle to become a historian was far from over, he had found a side door that would give him entry to the history profession. For someone of his ethnic background, geographic setting, and limited financial resources to have come even this far was strong testimony to his determination and qualities of mind. But his accomplishments were also due in no small measure to the encouragement that he received from people like Father Elliott Ross and Eugene C. Barker who guided his steps during these formative years. Barker, in particular, through his example and counsel had helped direct the young Castañeda along the path that eventually led to a career as university teacher and scholar. Carlos's training was not over, but his dedication to history would never be stronger.

---

41 Barker to Castañeda, Feb. 19, 1925, Barker Papers.
42 Castañeda to Barker, March 4, 1925, *ibid;* Gonzales, "Castañeda," 4.

Patrón Leadership at the Crossroads: Southern Colorado in the Late Nineteenth Century

William B. Taylor and
Elliott West

*Mr. Taylor is an associate professor of history in the
University of Colorado and Mr. West is an assistant professor of history in the University of Texas, Arlington.*

ALTHOUGH HISTORIANS have given increasing attention to the
study of ethnic minorities, many gaps remain in the story of Mexican Americans and the places they have inhabited. In surveys of
the Southwest, for example, the meager historical information on
the early settlement of southern Colorado often is superficial, misleading, or wrong.[1] The history of Mexican-American communities
in particular has been neglected. We know little of their local
politics, their changing problems, and their interaction with state
and national societies. The truncated Mexican-American past represents more than a gap in ethnic history, for it leaves us with an
incomplete understanding of all facets of regional and national life
influenced by Spanish-surnamed Americans. In the literature on

---

[1] For example, a recent historical geography of the southwest comes to the misleading conclusion that bicultural cities like Durango, Alamosa, and Walsenburg were
prototypes of Mexican American settlement in Colorado because Mexican Americans
were "everywhere adjuncts of Anglo activities" and because there was no "Hispano-
dominated countryside." D. W. Meinig, *Southwest: Three Peoples in Geographical
Change, 1600–1970* (New York, 1971), 124–125.

rural society and politics after the Civil War, for instance, the most detailed study of farm tenantry includes material on the south, north, and midwest but none on the Mexican-American Southwest.[2]

Our purpose is to describe the structure of rural society in two parts of southern Colorado where Mexican Americans constituted an important part of the population at the end of the nineteenth century and the beginning of the twentieth century. By "structure" we mean the complex pattern of relationships that held people together in an identifiable community and connected them to the larger society outside.[3] Las Animas County, along the New Mexico border east of the Culebra Mountains, and Saguache County, at the northern tip of the San Luis Valley, are the examples for this study. Although by 1885 Anglos dominated the towns of these counties, roughly two-thirds of the heads of families of the countryside in Las Animas and about a third of those in Saguache were Spanish-surnamed.[4] For primary evidence we rely heavily on the diaries of John Lawrence, founder of Saguache, the Colorado Writer's Project transcripts of interviews with early settlers of southern Colorado, and the personal papers and correspondence of José Urbano Vigil, an influential Las Animas County politician from the 1890s to 1915.[5] The Vigil correspondence contains several hundred letters from the founders and citizens of small Mexican-American communities west of the city of Trinidad.

While southern Colorado was not settled permanently by Mexicans before the Treaty of Guadalupe Hidalgo in 1848, the flow of settlers north from New Mexico after 1850 should not be confused with the westward movement of European immigrants. Taking ship

---

2 William B. Bizzell, *Farm Tenantry in the United States* (Lubbock, Texas, 1921).

3 The concept of social structure is presented in A. R. Radcliffe-Brown's *Structure and Function in Primitive Society* (Glencoe, Ill., 1952). For a recent application of the principle of structure and use of ideal types, see Robert G. Keith, "Encomienda, Hacienda, and Corregimiento in Spanish America: A Structural Analysis," *Hispanic American Historical Review*, LI (1971), 431–446.

4 Schedules of the Colorado State Census of 1885, File 158, rolls 6 and 8, Microcopies of Records in the National Archives, copy in Norlin Library, University of Colorado, Boulder.

5 John Lawrence diaries, typescript, Western Historical Collection, University of Colorado, Boulder (hereafter cited as JL); Colorado Writers' Project, two volumes of typescript for Las Animas County, Colorado State Historical Society, Denver (hereafter cited as CWP Las Animas); José Urbano Vigil Papers, Box 1, Western Historical Collection, University of Colorado, Boulder (hereafter cited as JUV).

to America often meant an abrupt break with the past. In contrast, the Mexican-American settlements in southern Colorado formed the northward thrust of a cultural tradition—a natural, almost involuntary step.[6] Unlike other nineteenth-century minorities, rural Mexican Americans could challenge the imperatives of national culture with separate rights deriving from land ownership and a set of values firmly rooted in the land prior to incorporation into the United States. The Indian frontier and the natural setting of Colorado contributed to the character of the new settlements, but the core culture was that of Mexico's northern frontier. The new Colorado communities extended the rural society of New Mexico onto lands marked out for settlement by the Mexican government in the 1840s.

One set of core values brought to southern Colorado centered on the person of the patrón.[7] The patrón relationship amounted to a personal dependence and mutual obligation between a large landowner and the peasants living on or near his property. In its pure form the patrón-based society of the Mexican frontier approached a static self-sufficiency with local demands for food, clothing, and other necessities being satisfied by the resources of the landowner. The patrón provided the only important connection with the world outside the community. He sold the local produce and supplied virtually all goods brought into the community. The patrón also served as the political spokesman and embodied local law, acting as an informal legislator, policeman, and judge.

Privilege was linked with obligation in this social arrangement.

---

6 Carey McWilliams develops the idea of a cultural continuum extending from northern Mexico into the American Southwest in *North from Mexico: The Spanish-Speaking People of the United States* (New York, 1949).

7 The southern portion of Colorado's San Luis Valley represents a somewhat different set of values. While patrones and sharecroppers were not lacking, there was more emphasis on community property (especially irrigation ditches), small private farms, and less social differentiation. (See the San Luis Vega Improvement Company Papers, Colorado State Historical Society; Olibama López, "Spanish Heritage in the San Luis Valley" [M.A. thesis, University of Denver, 1942]; Alvar W. Carlson, "Rural Settlement Patterns in the San Luis Valley: A Comparative Study," *Colorado Magazine*, XLIV [1967], 113–120). Clark S. Knowlton divides the patrón system into two classes: village leaders and landholding patrones. We would expect to find his "village patrón" in the southern portion of the San Luis Valley. Our description of the ideal type is similar to Knowlton's landholding patrón. Clark S. Knowlton, "Patrón-Peón Patterns Among Spanish Americans of New Mexico," *Social Forces*, XLI (1962), 12–17.

In exchange for the personal loyalty of his people, the patrón assumed a number of social duties on their behalf. His traditional mission was to protect and help those who depended upon him and always take their side even against the law and the state. He owed his people relative security at the subsistence level and to this end often loaned them cash, seed, animals, and clothing. In short, the essential link in social and economic relations was personal fealty. For his part, the patrón offered protection and aid while those who came under his protection contributed service and personal support.

A closed patrón society would function best in an isolated rural setting where the loyalties of the community to the patrón were complete and free from the external pressures of a market economy or socio-political authority beyond the patrón and local traditions. Participants in a patrón society would identify strongly with the family and the local community. Only secondarily, if at all, would the residents place themselves within the larger society as Mexicans, Americans, or Mexican Americans. This description of the patrón society is not meant to summarize the reality of the rural Southwest in 1900. We use it as a standard or ideal type against which to examine the variety of rural patterns in Mexican-American society, their changes, and their continuities. Patrón society in a relatively pure and static form could be found only on the immense haciendas of northern Mexico before the Revolution of 1910 where a firmly entrenched system of debt peonage prevailed.[8]

Measured against this ideal type, patrón society in Las Animas and Saguache around 1900 reveals a rich variety of structural patterns: small, isolated communities which approached complete dependence on a Spanish-speaking patrón; rural communities dependent upon an acculturated Anglo leader who understood the obligations as well as the privileges of the patrón relationship; urbanized Mexican-American patrones who lived in the southern city of Trinidad but maintained close personal ties and mutual respon-

8 The following works examine the hacienda as a social entity in northern Mexico: Francois Chevalier, *La formation des grands domaines au Mexique: terre et société aux XVIe–XVIIe siècles* (Paris, 1952); Charles H. Harris, *The Sánchez Navarros: A Socio-Economic Study of a Coahuilan Latifundio, 1846–1853* (Chicago, 1964); and Eric Wolf and Sidney Mintz, "Haciendas and Plantations in Middle America and the Antilles," *Social and Economic Studies*, VI (1957), 380–412.

sibilities with rural patrones and their own rural communities; and political patrones representing the south but attached to the style of life and politics in the state capital at Denver.

The most complete form of patrón society was to be found in the remote plaza settlements west of Trinidad. These compact communities often took the form of a large, walled rectangle with an open courtyard or plaza in the center.[9] A plaza community often was named for its founder and first patrón (e.g., Madrid, Torres, Vigil). The early plazas of the 1860s may have originated with one or more extended families. Initial settlement by a father and his adult sons, brothers, cousins, and their families would seem to explain why the early plazas were called "Los Medina," "Los Gonzales," "Los Tijera," "Los Madrid," and so forth (the Medinas, etc.).[10] Casimiro Barela suggests such settlement of the first plazas by extended families with his description of how the Barela family plaza town began in 1866:

On getting back home [New Mexico], I told my father and brothers of the fine lands and grass around Trinidad. I proposed that we form a colony and move there. This suggestion was adopted and my father's family all came. . . . The village of Trinidad did not appeal to us, and we located on the San Francisco Creek.[11]

The power and influence of the plaza patrón rested on an economic foundation as well as a cultural tradition. The patrón typically was the wealthiest man in the community. He usually owned the townsite, buildings, and much of the arable and grazing land in the immediate vicinity.[12] The land and part of the patrón's livestock might be rented or let out on shares to Spanish-surname residents of the plaza.[13] It was largely through him that residents of a plaza participated in county and state affairs. He monopolized local com-

---

9 Hugh and Evelyn Burnett, "Madrid Plaza," *Colorado Magazine*, XLII (1965), 224–237. Patrones who appear in the Vigil correspondence include J. M. García of Delagua, J. R. Córdova and family of Weston, J. L. Torres of Torres, and J. B. Aragón of Strong. Other communities west of Trinidad are mentioned in the Vigil papers and may also have been patrón societies: Primero, Segundo, Tercio, Aguilar, Hastings, Gulnare, Stonewall, and Esperanza.

10 CWP Las Animas, Vol. 1, p. 85; Morris Taylor, *Trinidad, Colorado Territory* (Pueblo, Colo., 1966), 26.

11 CWP Las Animas, Vol. 2, pp. 56–57.

12 CWP Las Animas, Vol. 1, p. 160; JUV, *passim*.

13 JUV estate papers, 1915; Julio Chacón to Vigil, April 17, 1905, JUV.

merece and provided virtually all goods and services not produced at home. Typically, he ran the only general store in town as well as the local bar and dance hall.[14] One resourceful patrón even bottled his own patent remedy, "La Sanadora," thereby eliminating the outside middle man.[15] Strong personal dependence upon the patrón often extended beyond land tenure and trade to credit at the general store or cash loans to meet emergencies. Letters in the Vigil Collection record small loans for such emergencies as medical care, land litigation, and delinquent debts to outsiders. This voluntary economic dependence was cemented by bonds of personal trust and family sentiment. If not a blood relation, the patrón usually was godfather to a child of each plaza family, making him a *compadre* and member of the extended family.[16]

In exchange for his paternalistic care, the patrón advised and represented local citizens in their business affairs and legal problems. In addition he virtually monopolized political influence. Because loyalty flowed directly to the patrón rather than to the state or to political parties, the plaza leader could control local politics with some confidence. Political organization of these rural communities at the county level amounted to little more than the division of plaza patrones into Democratic and Republican camps. For example, in Precinct 3 of Las Animas County which in 1912 included Torres and smaller outlying settlements, the Democrats held a comfortable majority of registered voters and ninety-four percent of the Democrats had Spanish surnames.[17] It is no surprise to find that the leading citizen and businessman of Torres, J. L. Torres, was an active Democrat.

The political contacts of the plaza patrón outside his community provided him with a greater sense of ethnic identification than would be found among his dependents. Several letters in the Vigil Collection divide Las Animas society into two large groups: "amer-

---

14 Letterheads of J. R. Córdova and J. L. Torres: "Dealer in General Merchandise, Weston, Colo.," "Dealer in General Merchandise, Hay, Grain, Etc." When J. L. Torres sold a ranch to a Mr. Schomburg, the buyer had to promise not to open a general store or bar in the Torres plaza. Torres to Vigil, April 19, 1902, JUV.

15 Letterhead of J. R. Córdova, *ibid*.

16 Jacabo Duran to Vigil, April 8, 1905, *ibid*.

17 Registration list in JUV Papers. Of the 224 registered Democrats, 210 had Spanish surnames. On the Republican side, there were 87 Anglos and Italians, and 67 Mexican Americans.

icanos" (Anglo Americans) and "nuestra raza" ("our people," Mexican Americans).[18] The ethnic awareness of the patrones also could surface in stereotypes of other ethnic groups. For example, local Italians were labelled "degos and other vagabonds."[19] Ethnic feelings were most likely to appear at election time. Campaign gifts sometimes contained the proviso that the money be used to support "Mexican candidates."[20] Patrones were acutely aware of the "vendido" or political "sell out." One Democratic patrón accused his Mexican-American brothers who voted Republican in 1900 of "hoping to acquire blue eyes."[21] State and county political organizers who failed to appreciate the importance of the patrón contributed to this solidarity at the polls. The frustrations of Judge John Moore, a leading Democrat at the Las Animas convention in 1904, illustrates the point:

Judge John Moore made a rousing speech, and addressed some of his remarks specially to the Mexicans present, saying that some of the leaders think that because they name a man, the delegates should fall in like sheep and vote for that man. . . . Casimiro Barela said that Judge Moore had made some insulting remarks which reflected upon his Mexican friends.[22]

By 1900 pressures from outside were beginning to threaten the isolation and self-sufficiency of the plaza settlements and the independent power of the patrón. Mines, railroads, and the timber industry produced new landowners, new jobs, and a steady flow of non-Mexican immigrants into southern Colorado. In 1900 the Rocky Mountain Timber Company (a wholly-owned subsidiary of the Colorado Fuel and Iron Company) acquired from the Maxwell Land Grant Company a wide strip along the southern border of Colorado including lands near the Vigil and Rincón plazas. Mexican Americans who, through their patrones, had leased these lands from the Maxwell Company were forced to renegotiate their leases. The timber firm insisted that the land be leased only on shares, thus

18 Juan M. García to Vigil (undated); J. R. Córdova to Vigil, May 7, 1901; unsigned letter to Vigil, June 10, 1910, JUV.
19 J. L. Torres to Vigil, Oct. 9, 1902, *ibid.*
20 J. L. Torres to Vigil, Oct. 13, 1912, *ibid.*
21 J. R. Córdova to Vigil, May 7, 1901, *ibid.*
22 CWP Las Animas, Vol. 1, p. 132.

forcing families off the land or severing the direct lines of fealty between patrón and peasant.[23]

At about the same time, new coal mines appeared west of Trinidad. In 1900 the Colorado Fuel and Iron Company began large-scale operations at Primero; in 1901 another new mine was started near the Torres plaza.[24] The mines dealt a severe blow to the isolation and economic self-sufficiency of the plazas. Mine operators acquired a right of way across the Madrid plaza lands which they used as a refuse site for mine tailings.[25] Erosion, diminished productivity on the land, and the attractions of wage labor in the mines gradually led to the abandonment of this plaza town. The decline of a plaza meant the decline of the local patrón. Wage labor reduced the personal economic ties between patrón and peasant. Landless families who remained in the plazas came to expect cash wages rather than a portion of the crop for their labors.[26] The presence of outsiders, especially the Italians who came to work the coal mines, drastically reduced the political power of the patrón. The new arrivals felt no binding loyalty to the patrón and often followed the mineowners' lead at election time.[27]

The story of John Lawrence, sheep rancher, merchant, and political leader of the San Luis Valley, helps explain both the establishment and decline of the patrón's position, for Lawrence was a traditional figure who played well the role of the patrón yet actively promoted development and change deadly to the older social system of his region.

Swept up in the rush for Colorado gold, Lawrence arrived in Denver in 1859 at the age of twenty-four, and, after brief careers as a miner, rancher, and freighter, moved in 1861 to Conejos, Colorado Territory. Lawrence learned Spanish quickly and soon was acting as interpreter between earlier settlers from New Mexico and Anglo newcomers. In February 1867, accompanied by three Mexican Americans who were to become his sharecroppers, he moved northward to homestead in the upper San Luis Valley.[28] There he

---

23 Ira B. Gale to Vigil, Nov. 19, 1901, JUV. J. R. Córdova mentioned the eviction of six families southwest of Weston in a letter to Vigil dated December 17, 1901, *ibid.*
24 JUV records of Vigil dated 1901, *ibid.*
25 Burnett and Burnett, "Madrid Plaza," 236.
26 Ramón Domínguez to Vigil, Oct. 5, 1902, JUV.
27 J. L. Torres to Vigil, Oct. 9, 1902, *ibid.*
28 Beryl McAdow, *Land of Adoption* (Boulder, Colo., 1970), 7–11.

remained to build a minor empire of several thousand acres valued at $31,000 by developers who tried unsuccessfully to buy him out two decades later.[29]

Lawrence was scarcely settled before he eagerly, even aggressively, began to assume the obligations of a patrón. When he discovered a lack of concern about a recently deceased neighbor, Juan Borrego, Lawrence provided materials for a coffin, selected a plot, then laid the dead man to rest on a knoll that became the town cemetery.[30] Within two years Lawrence's Spanish-surname neighbors were looking to him to write personal and business letters and were granting him power of attorney to handle legal squabbles and to compose documents.[31] The bachelor held his share of fandangos and attended many others, though the revelry occasionally meant a day off for all hands due to fatigue.[32] The relative ease and speed with which Lawrence assumed his position suggests that nationality was not a prerequisite for the role of patrón. An Anglo willing to assume traditional obligations received in return the acceptance and deference due a man of his position.

Lawrence also developed quickly the economic relationships typical of a patrón. From the time he arrived with three sharecroppers, he provided seed, implements, and his own physical help at planting and harvest in return for a portion, usually half, of the produce. Lawrence would measure off a homestead for his workers, then file the proper papers, pay any fees, and aid in building a dwelling as part of the bargain.[33] Realizing that the influence of a patrón often depended on the intimacy of frequent personal contact, Lawrence built the homes of workers or renters as near his own dwelling as possible.[34] The work of clearing brush, irrigation, and harvesting apparently was shared by the patrón and his renter, though later when Lawrence bought a horse-drawn thresher he charged for its use.[35] Frequently Lawrence deducted any debts of money or supplies and then bought what remained of the renter's

---

29 JL June 20, 1887.
30 JL March 11, 1867.
31 JL March 14, 1869, Dec. 12, 1868, Jan. 17, 1869.
32 JL July 9, 10, 11, and 18, 1868.
33 JL March 7, Aug. 14, 1867, March 19, 1871.
34 "Renter" will refer to a person farming or herding on a share basis.
35 JL July 11, Oct. 19, May 4, 1867, Oct. 18, 1869.

produce.[36] Payment might also include services, such as asking for the hand of a local belle on behalf of a renter and, should she accept, sponsoring a wedding and reception.[37]

By the mid-1870s, Lawrence had discovered a more lucrative occupation for his renters, and, by 1880, mention of farming had all but disappeared from his diary. Instead, sheep were loaned to renters, who cared for and sheared them in return for half of the wool and newborn lambs. Lawrence's shift to this tenant herding, or *partido* system, corresponded with the phenomenal increase in sheep herding in New Mexico during the 1870s.[38] Once sheep were sheared, wool was carried to a nearby railhead, Villa Grove or Del Norte, and sold or signed over to an agent who handled its transport and marketing in the East.[39] As much as 17,000 pounds of wool from Lawrence sheep rolled out of the valley in such annual shipments.

Nor was Lawrence's income limited to *partido* and sharecropping arrangements. From the start he loaned money and supplies to his renters, and in 1896 he became senior partner in the firm of Lawrence and Williams, which emerged as the county's largest hardware store.[40] Renters naturally secured what goods they needed from this establishment. Interest varied on supplies bought on credit, but renters often ended the year out of debt.[41] In making cash loans Lawrence was scrupulous not to charge a higher rate of interest than he paid at a Del Norte bank, two percent a month.[42] As the major source of supplies and credit for his renters, Lawrence might have profited much more than he did from this near monopolistic system. Yet such arrangements indicate that a sense of obligation and concern tempered his desire for gain.

Our impression of Lawrence's feeling of responsibility is strengthened by his social activities. As a legal adviser he drew up wills, acted as interpreter in court, informed officials of crimes against

36 JL Oct. 21, 1867.
37 JL Dec. 4, 1868.
38 Nancie L. Gonzales, *The Spanish-Americans of New Mexico: A Heritage of Pride* (Albuquerque, 1969), 47–48.
39 JL June 14, 1883, May 18, 1885.
40 McAdow, *Land of Adoption*, 18.
41 JL Feb. 22, 1871, July 11, 1892, Dec. 12, 1902.
42 JL Jan. 6, 1876.

his renters, and served as an unofficial arbiter in disputes.[43] He celebrated at weddings and paid his respects beside sick beds and at wakes. A round of whiskey awaited those who came to serenade him on San Juan's day (June 24), and visitors, particularly frequent during winter doldrums, fared well by his food, drink, and hospitality.[44] No one seeking work would be denied. In his final diary entry, made a few weeks before he died of a heart attack in 1907, Lawrence told of assigning part of a renter's flock of sheep to a destitute herder.[45]

Lawrence's social acceptance of his Mexican-American neighbors is indicated by his marriage in 1895 to Julia Vigil Woodson, the widow of his former partner, James Woodson. During his final years he lived with his wife's nephew, Daniel Vigil, and Vigil's wife, Martina, an orphan Lawrence had taken in when she was a young girl.[46] Such close bonds made him acutely aware of discrimination against Spanish-surname residents by Anglos who came to the San Luis Valley in increasing numbers. When a renter's daughter died of diptheria, Lawrence wrote with disgust of her treatment: "[D]octors have no more care or sympathy for the sick than a coyote for a rabbit, . . . if [he is] poor, a dead Mexican is as good as a live one to them."[47] Anglo control of cattle ranching and Mexican Americans' predominance among sheepherders added an aggravating cultural dimension to the economic conflict between these industries. In 1902, a herder, Perfecto Chaves, was shot to death in an incident many interpreted as part of a terror campaign to drive sheepmen from the county. When a jury freed a cowboy, Tom Tucker, on the charge, Lawrence was not surprised, for

This was expected by me, as it was race prejudice, for in the nearly 36 years . . . the county has been organized, the[re] never has been a case where a Mexican has accused an American of a crime, or where the American commited the crime against the Mexican but what the American has gone clear, and for the same time there has only been one case

---

[43] JL Dec. 8, 1896, Nov. 11, 1878, March 9, 1890, July 11, 1900, Dec. 27, 1872, Jan. 31, 1873.
[44] JL April 5, 1870, Jan. 3, 1890, Aug. 20, 1890, Aug. 26, 1883, June 24, 1874.
[45] JL Dec. 4, 1906.
[46] JL Dec. 25, 1895; McAdow, *Land of Adoption*, 25–27.
[47] JL Jan. 13 and 14, 1904.

where an American has accused a Mexican of a crime, or the crime has been against an American but what the Mexican has been found guilty and sent to the penetentiary.[48]

Deference shown by Lawrence toward those looking to him as patrón appears most clearly in his attitudes and actions regarding religion. Workers were allowed time off during holy week and on other religious holidays. Lawrence invited priests to say mass in his house, and when services were held elsewhere he often took the renters' families by wagon.[49] Yet he admitted in his will that he honored no God and defined himself as an infidel.[50] Whether consciously playing the role of patrón or acting from genuine sympathy, he showed a sensitivity to the place of religion in the lives of his renters and workers that was essential to his acceptance and success.

Such close economic and social relationships bestowed on Lawrence impressive political power. A Democrat all his adult life except for a brief Populist flirtation, Lawrence worked doggedly for his party in a strongly Republican county and served as delegate to the state Democratic convention and as a member of the state central committee. That his prestige was sufficient to outweigh partisanship is shown by his election at various times as state representative, mayor of Saguache, and school board secretary. In his political struggles, Lawrence's position as patrón served him well. Election eve invariably found him campaigning among Mexican Americans or organizing meetings and dances for them. Renters and laborers were carried to town to vote or to attend conventions.[51] Even opponents conceded that the rancher controlled 150 "Mexican" votes, a political following Lawrence's friends explained by his concern for those who looked to him for help and leadership: "The recipients of his bounty are many and to their credit be it said they are grateful. That is the secret of John Lawrence's strength with the 'poor Mexicans' as some flippantly call them."[52] Lawrence's election as state representative in 1898 indicates the extent and nature of his appeal. After consolidating his support among Mexican American acquaintances, he won by five votes in the county

48 JL Oct. 27, 1902.
49 JL Oct. 1, 1868, March 25, 1869, July 10, 1869, Oct. 11, 1876.
50 McAdow, *Land of Adoption*, 30.
51 JL Sept. 1, 1868, Oct. 6, 1879, Nov. 6, 1883, Nov. 1, 1884.
52 *Saguache Crescent*, Oct. 29, 1896, Oct. 27, 1898.

total, 713 to 708, while carrying his own precinct, 104 to 8.[53] Though the precise ethnic makeup of his precinct cannot be determined, comments in the local newspaper and entries in Lawrence's diary suggest that most of those ballots came from renters, work hands, and others who recognized the rancher as their social, economic, and political leader.[54]

Yet if Lawrence exhibited many characteristics typical of the patrón, his other activities showed a different side of the man. He strove to develop his region and to profit by its growth. During his early years in the area, he aggressively sought contracts to supply food to mines, military forts, and the southern Ute agency.[55] To facilitate such trade and to improve transportation in general, Lawrence chartered, surveyed, helped build, and served as trustee on several toll roads in the area.[56] The rancher served as midwife and zealous guardian for his adopted home, writing the charter of Saguache, then campaigning to make it the county seat. He also invested heavily in the less successful town of Sedwick—at one time he owned 2,800 lots—and did his best to encourage its growth.[57] When rich strikes were made in the mountains around his valley, Lawrence bought part interest in several mines and devoted much time to their development, though he met with only limited success.[58] Agricultural and pastoral pursuits were not neglected, however, for he actively promoted local, regional, and national organizations of farmers and stock raisers.[59]

Such interests typify not a patrón but a capitalist and speculator bent on growth, as rapid and lucrative as possible, for his locality. The authority and influence of the classic patrón relationship depended upon isolation, for in a self-contained, tightly integrated community such a leader's economic power went virtually unchallenged.[60] Growth weakened bonds of personal dependence and undermined traditional customs and values. Yet Lawrence the patrón

---

53 *Ibid.,* Nov. 17, 1898.
54 *Ibid.,* Oct. 27, 1898; JL Oct. 22, 1898.
55 JL May 8, 1868, Nov. 19, 1871, Nov. 7, 1875, May 3, 1879.
56 JL Jan. 7, 1873, April 12, 1875, June 8, 1875, May 30, 1884.
57 JL Aug. 7, Nov. 2, Nov. 29, 1873, April 17, 1882.
58 JL Jan. 9, 1882, May 8, 1891.
59 JL April 9, 1872, Jan. 12, 1900, March 8, 1902.
60 U.S. Department of Agriculture, Bureau of Agricultural Economics, *Culture of a Contemporary Rural Community: El Cerrito, New Mexico,* by Olen Leonard and C. P. Loomis (Washington, D.C., 1941), 9, 70.

displayed the dedication of an ardent regional booster and economic expansionist. Always his outlook and interests transcended the local complex of relationships that bestowed on him impressive power and position. He was a man of two worlds: the static society of the patrón and his people and the entrepreneurial realm of capital and development.

In his sensitive adaptation to a Mexican-American society, Lawrence departed from the pervasive belief in self-help and intolerance of alien cultures which were common in late nineteenth-century America.[61] Lawrence's distance from the American mainstream hinges on a lack of ethnocentrism which allowed him to apply one set of standards to his own career and another to the regional society of Saguache. On a personal level, he pursued the traditional Anglo goal of capital accumulation through the economics of boosterism and control of commerce. But in his relationships with the Mexican Americans of Saguache, Lawrence replaced belief in self-help with the more communal values of mutual aid and responsibility which lay at the foundation of the patrón system. His adjustment to Mexican-American ways is striking, although not at odds with his personal goals of wealth and influence.

Several factors might account for Lawrence's flexibility. An orphan who had lived virtually as a vagabond from the age of fourteen until his arrival in Colorado, he was not imbued with the full range of attitudes of his mother culture. The Anglo family has proved an effective transmitter of values, but Lawrence came to Saguache a bachelor and enjoyed more leeway in adapting to his new surroundings than would a man with a wife and children. Furthermore, Lawrence settled in southern Colorado before the urbanized Anglo frontier penetrated the Mexican-American areas. Like the early merchants of New Mexico, he modified his interpersonal behavior to fit the cultural patterns of the majority rather than attempting to remake local life styles single-handedly. Communities of Anglo families, in which personal and public values were constantly reinforced, later would come in overwhelming numbers to challenge the

---

[61] For a recent appraisal of the belief in self-help, see Kermit Vanderbilt, "The Gospel of Self-Help and Success in the Gilded Age," in Robert Skotheim and Michael McGiffert, eds., *American Social Thought: Sources and Interpretations* (2 vols., Reading, Mass., 1972), II, 5–117.

social ways of southern Colorado. Whatever the reasons for his flexibility, Lawrence was a transitional figure in his attitudes and sympathies as well as in his economic interests. His system of values was a selective composite of the different cultures he confronted.

While Lawrence and some plaza leaders established their position as patrones in the traditional rural setting, other leading plaza families in Las Animas County sometimes chose to live in the city of Trinidad. Trinidad attracted many educated sons of plaza patrones, who found the urban setting better suited to their skills as lawyers, teachers, insurance representatives, realtors, and journalists. Those who possessed a measure of wealth and who took on the privileges and obligations of political office became patrones of a special type. With one foot in the city and the other still rooted in the rural plaza, these men comprised a dual elite, providing a bridge between town and countryside.

The career and structural relationships of one dual patrón can be examined in some detail in the personal papers of José Urbano Vigil of Vigil and Trinidad.[62] Vigil turned his education and training as a school teacher to good account in Trinidad from the 1880s to his death in 1915 by serving as a notary public, county clerk, director of the Trinidad Publishing Company, member of the Democratic state central committee, and county chairman of the Democratic party. With personal horizons and political contacts much wider than those of the rural patrones, he was more expansive and inclined to take greater risks. Vigil tried his hand at a number of entrepreneurial ventures, including publishing, merchandising, land speculation, and supplying stage ponies and hay. In 1914 he also devised an apparently unsuccessful scheme to sell cattle south of the border during the Mexican Revolution. High state officials curried his favor with obsequious letters and invitations to speeches

---

[62] Although Vigil's career is by far the best documented, the careers of three other dual patrones can be sketched: Teodore Abeyta, José R. Aguilar, and J. M. Madrid. Abeyta, a sheep rancher who established permanent residence in Trinidad, served as undersheriff in 1885 and county assessor from 1898 to 1902. His brother, Vivián, was a state legislator and county commissioner in the 1890s. Aguilar founded Aguilar, Colorado, and served as county commissioner in the 1890s. Madrid, born in 1902, moved from the Madrid plaza to Trinidad in 1905, became a realtor and insurance agent, served in the state legislature in 1902, was county superintendent of schools from 1904 to 1912, and was elected state senator in 1932. CWP Las Animas, Vol. 1, pp. 76–88.

and dinners in Denver. He also belonged to at least three organizations which broadened his social contacts: Knights of Pythias, Association of the Sacred Heart, and La Sociedad de Beneficencia Mutua.

While Vigil had left the rural setting to take up publishing, the merchant trade, and politics in Trinidad, his correspondence suggests that he continued to maintain close ties with many plaza communities, especially the town of Vigil. Vigil's rural interests included several ranches and farming sites near his home plaza. The ranches were regularly rented, and Vigil's herd of goats was assigned on shares to at least three different individuals.[63] Two of the renters refer to Vigil as *padrino* (godfather) or *compadre*. From the correspondence it appears that Vigil retained many of the obligations as well as the wealth and influence of a rural patrón. He received letters from residents of Vigil pouring out their troubles, seeking small loans and legal or personal advice, and asking him to fill out forms, witness a land possession, cosign a bank note, or make a homestead claim.

Perhaps the most important of Vigil's rural ties were with the plaza patrones. The bulk of his correspondence came from leading citizens of the small communities west of Trinidad. As county chairman of the Democratic party Vigil cultivated the support of influential Mexican Americans throughout the county and corresponded frequently about elections and candidates. In this sense he was a political patrón, perhaps the only consistent link between many rural communities and county and state political leaders. At this level, too, obligation accompanied support. Local patrones resorted to Vigil in disputes with the railroads or for legal advice and personal favors.

In the city the ties of personal dependence naturally were less complete than in the plaza. Except for his store, where fifty-seven of the sixty individuals indebted to him had Spanish surnames, and occasional emergency loans, dependence hinged on Vigil's ability to use political influence rather than economic power for special favors and patronage. Friends asked him to help them to secure teaching

---

63 Estate papers, 1915, JUV.

positions, appointments at foreign consulates, special privileges for prison inmates, free train passes, and extension of loans.

Politics, family ties, and personal influence merged in Vigil's political style, which retained the personal quality of dependence and responsibility characteristic of the patrón relationship. Political allies like the plaza patrones were his "compadres" who expected of Vigil the loyalty and generosity of a brother. Vigil acted as if his name and personal position were sufficient to win the day for his supporters in their personal affairs and grievances. Sometimes he succeeded, especially when minor patronage, teaching positions, and free train passes were at issue. Vigil's style was less successful in matters of law or in dealings with the railroads. For example, his efforts to secure payment from the Colorado and Wyoming Railway Company for cattle belonging to J. R. Córdova which were killed on the tracks met with a direct rebuff from the railroad's lawyer: ". . . to pay the claim on the ground that this party is related to and allied to prominent citizens does not appeal to me as fair and just, and that the poorest man living along the line deserves more consideration than one who is able to stand the loss."[64]

In exchange for the patronage and influence which came to him as the local Democratic leader, Vigil gave up a degree of independence and responsibility to his people. Apparently he fulfilled the expectations of those Democrats who believed that his first loyalty was to the party. In 1913, one state politician said of Vigil: "He has kept himself a poor man fighting for the Democratic Party in the face of discouragement and defeat and with traitors in his own camp where he could have been a rich man had he let the Party go."[65] Loyalty to the party meant supporting the party's candidates, few of whom were Mexican Americans or took the Spanish-speaking constituency into account. As the mines and railroads gained political influence in the south, Vigil's political position became more difficult. The rural communities, suspicious of collusion between politicians and the new industries, lost faith in their elected repre-

---

[64] Fred Harrington to Vigil, March 26, 1904, *ibid*.
[65] Dr. Wycoff, quoted by Fred W. Clark in a letter to Vigil, March 28, 1913, *ibid*.

sentatives. J. R. Córdova put these sentiments into words in 1902:
"I do not have the least interest in politics this year because, to tell
the truth, our legislators work only for their own benefit. As soon as
we elect them they give themselves over body and soul to the corporations and companies. They do nothing for the good of the people who elected them."[66]

The Mexican-American men of influence furthest removed from
the pure patrón relationship were the state politicians. Casimiro
Barela, Colorado's most famous Mexican American of the late nineteenth century and one of only sixteen men to have his countenance
immortalized in the dome of the State Capitol, provides an interesting example. Hard upon his arrival from northern New Mexico
in 1866, Barela began his public career in Las Animas County, first
as a justice of the peace, and later as county sheriff, county assessor,
county treasurer, and county judge.[67] By 1871 he had launched his
career in state politics as a representative to the territorial legislature. He was elected to the state senate in 1876 where he served
continuously until his death in 1920. He attended two Democratic
national conventions as a Colorado delegate and also served as the
Denver consul for Mexico and Costa Rica. Barela combined politics with economic influence. He ranked among the largest landowners and leading entrepreneurs of southern Colorado. His enterprises included large shares of the San Luis Valley Railroad and the
American Savings Bank of Trinidad, cattle and sheep ranches in
the San Francisco Valley, and a "merchandising and forwarding"
business at Trinidad and El Moro which operated out of the Barela
Block, an imposing office building in Trinidad.[68]

In his political as well as his business style, Barela had acquired
mainstream American values. One measure of his acceptability in
Anglo society was his membership in organizations which systematically excluded Mexican Americans. Barela was the only Spanish-
surname member of the Trinidad Chamber of Commerce in 1888.
He also was one of only three Mexican Americans included in the

---

[66] J. R. Córdova to Vigil, Sept. 21, 1902, *ibid.*

[67] José E. Fernández, *Cuarenta años de legislador o biografía del Senador Casimiro
Barela* (Trinidad, 1911); Wilbur F. Stone, ed., *History of Colorado* (4 vols., Chicago,
1918), III, 666–670; James H. Baker, ed., *History of Colorado* (5 vols., Denver, 1927),
V, 439–440.

[68] Stone, *History of Colorado*, III, 666–670; Baker, *History of Colorado*, V, 439–440;
Representative Men of Colorado in the Nineteenth Century (Denver, 1902), 16.

biographical dictionaries of Colorado published in the early 1900s. One biographer acclaimed him as a "wise and conscientious legislator"; another was impressed by his ability to "fuse Spanish elements into the highest type of American citizenship."[69] His regular re-election to the state senate was one sign of popularity, and he apparently claimed the loyal support of Mexican-American delegates to the Democratic party's county conventions (until he left the party in 1908) even though few of his political cohorts and proteges were Mexican Americans.

While personal magnetism and economic power may have been the twin keys to his long success in state politics, Barela consciously rejected the idea that he was a patrón to the Mexican Americans of Las Animas County. A revealing episode in 1899 suggests that he thought of himself as performing the same function as any other duly elected official. At a meeting of Mexican-American settlers at Torres, Colorado, Barela promised "relief to these poor people whose lands have been taken from them." When the settlers thanked him effusively and compared him to a father defending his children, he rejected the inference of paternalism and stressed that he was "simply doing what was required of a Senator."[70]

The complexity of the rural patrón's relationship with those around him perhaps can be understood more clearly if compared with a contemporary system in the American South. After the Civil War, planters often developed economic bonds with freed slaves which resembled those between the patrón and his dependents. Both systems depended largely upon the owner-sharecropper relationship, and, like the rural patrón, many planters doubled as merchants and loaned their dependents goods and cash in addition to supplies provided as part of the tenant contract.[71] Such similarities, however, should not obscure differences in the economic systems of the two regions. As homesteaders, for example, many rural Mexican Americans in Colorado technically owned their land, although they usually remained economically subservient to the patrón.

---

[69] Stone, *History of Colorado*, III, 666–670; Baker, *History of Colorado*, V, 439–440.
[70] J. L. Torres to Vigil, Dec. 18, 1899, JUV.
[71] Bizzell, *Farm Tenantry*, 211–217; Robert P. Brooks, *The Agrarian Revolution in Georgia, 1865–1912* (Madison, Wis., 1914), 60–67; Jacqueline Bull, "The General Merchant in the Economic History of the New South," *Journal of Southern History*, XVIII (1952), 37–40.

Parallels between the political relationships of the southern and southwestern systems are less apparent. In the immediate aftermath of Reconstruction, some southern whites who had held political and social leadership before the war did seem to accept Negro suffrage because they believed black people would vote according to the recommendations of their former masters. Thus, newly freed slaves hopefully would provide blocks of votes, much as the rural Mexican Americans supplied political power for the patrón.[72] Yet such attitudes never predominated among whites, and by 1900 most southern Negroes had lost what voting rights they had gained under Reconstruction.[73] As long as the patrón system remained, on the other hand, rural communities in Las Animas and Saguache seem to have willingly given their allegiance to the local leaders. Far from advocating disfranchisement, political leaders of southern Colorado encouraged participation by Mexican Americans, whom they regarded as a stable and predictable voting group.[74]

The two systems contrasted most glaringly in the area of social contacts. By the 1890s, the planter-cropper relationship and southern society in general rested upon a code of etiquette that governed virtually all circumstances of race relations and even defined proper attire and methods of addressing individuals.[75] Segregated by law in public, the owner and sharecropper rarely visited privately unless an emergency or death required it.[76] The patrón expected a

---

[72] Forrest G. Wood, "On Revising Reconstruction History: Negro Suffrage, White Disfranchisement, and Common Sense," *Journal of Negro History*, LI (1966), 102–103; George B. Tindall, "The Campaign for the Disfranchisement of Negroes in South Carolina," *Journal of Southern History*, XV (1949), 212–213.

[73] Among the more enlightening sources on this topic are Paul Lewinson, *Race, Class, and Party: A History of Negro Suffrage and White Politics in the South* (London, 1932); V. O. Key Jr., *Southern Politics in State and Nation* (New York, 1949); Tindall, "Disfranchisement in South Carolina," 212–234; William A. Mabry, "Disfranchisement of the Negro in Mississippi," *Journal of Southern History*, IV (1938), 318–333; Frank B. Williams, Jr., "The Poll Tax as a Suffrage Requirement in the South, 1870–1901," *Journal of Southern History*, XVIII (1952), 469–496.

[74] See, for example, *Saguache Chronicle*, Oct. 17, 1884.

[75] Bertram W. Doyle, *The Etiquette of Race Relations in the South: A Study in Social Control* (Port Washington, N.Y., 1968), chap. 10.

[76] There is disagreement over the time when a rigid system of race relations emerged in the South and the extent of racial contact during the years following the Civil War. Compare, for instance, C. Vann Woodward, *The Strange Career of Jim Crow* (Rev. ed., New York, 1966) with Joel Williamson, *After Slavery: The Negro in South Carolina During Reconstruction, 1861–1877* (Chapel Hill, 1965). In all such works, however, contact between planter and sharecropper would seem to be significantly more limited than between patrón and renter in the Southwest.

degree of deference from those below him, but social mobility, intermarriage, and personal ties between the groups were not uncommon.[77] Custom allowed, indeed demanded, contact between the patrón and his people not just at times of personal crisis and celebration but also at festivals and on holidays and for informal visits.

The key to the difference lies in the importance of race in the South. Southern custom could not tolerate intimacy of white owner and black worker; in the Southwest, patrón and dependent usually were of the same ethnic and cultural background. John Lawrence was an exception that proved the rule. An Anglo, he found acceptance once he assumed, eagerly and with sensitivity, the obligations of his position. His marriage and close personal ties among Mexican Americans illustrate that nationality counted less than attitude and acceptance of traditional mores.[78]

Despite similarities in the economic relationships of the two societies, therefore, other differences throw into relief important characteristics of Colorado's patrón system. The contrast in social relationships especially suggests the fundamental difference between a social structure based on shared values and one based on force. In addition to organizing economic life, the planter-cropper relationship of the South provided a mechanism of social control. In an effort to save the basis of the ante-bellum socio-economic life, southerners strove to retain the blacks' dependence upon their former masters after the war.[79] Sharecropping provided a suitable method, for owners or their overseers could keep close watch over the work and private activities of tenants and could use their economic position or even corporal punishment for control.[80] "Indeed," as one sympathizer of this arrangement has written, "the share system is not altogether incompatible with gang labor."[81] Though not all considered Negroes to be innately inferior, most white southerners believed that for the public good black people

---

[77] Olen Leonard, *The Role of the Land Grant in the Social Organization and Social Processes of a Spanish-American Village in New Mexico* (Ann Arbor, 1948), 118–119.

[78] Nor was Lawrence's an isolated case. See the list of twenty-two instances of intermarriage in early Las Animas County, Colorado, in CWP Las Animas, Vol. 1, p. 289.

[79] William E. Highsmith, "Some Aspects of Reconstruction in the Heart of Louisiana," *Journal of Southern History*, XIII (1947), 469, 476.

[80] Ray Stannard Baker, *Following the Color Line: American Negro Citizenship in the Progressive Era* (New York, 1964), 80–86; Bizzell, *Farm Tenantry*, 200–204; Brooks, *Agrarian Revolution in Georgia*, 60–67.

[81] Brooks, *Agrarian Revolution in Georgia*, 66.

should be kept in their subordinate position at least temporarily.[82]

By contrast, both the patrón and those depending on him seem to have accepted and defended their relationship. Each saw the advantage of his position; each recognized his duties. The purpose was not so much control of one group by another as maintenance of a life based on custom and tradition in which all members survived with dignity.[83] Similar to its southern counterpart in its economic arrangements, the patrón system differed in the allegiance of its participants and in the impulses that created and nurtured it.

By the turn of the century, this way of life was under siege. As elsewhere, the coming of the railroad altered the foundations of the region's social structure.[84] The bond of the railroad gradually integrated the isloated communities into a larger, Anglo-dominated world. On the Denver and Rio Grande came Anglo farmers, ranchers, and merchants who controlled an increasing share of the land and business of southern Colorado. Unlike Lawrence, the newcomers had little interest in investigating, much less adopting, the customs of a people they judged inferior; the web of traditon, so influential in isolation, faced disruption. Mostly Protestant, new arrivals were more concerned with converting or maligning Catholics than accepting them.[85] As a result, economic control gravitated to persons who wielded the power of a patrón without taking on the accompanying responsibilities. Impersonal relationships based on wages, profits, and credit replaced a system of reciprocal duties. A hard-nosed business mentality replaced mutual protection. New landowners such as the Rocky Mountain Timber Company felt justified in foreclosing on unpaid mortgages and overdue rents of their Mexican-American tenants. As the manager of the company explained after foreclosing on Lisardo Córdova's land near Weston in 1905, "In September and October he should have done as much

---

82 Guion G. Johnson, "Southern Paternalism toward Negroes after Emancipation," *Journal of Southern History,* XXIII (1957), 485–486.

83 As an indication of mutual trust and local acceptance of Lawrence's position, for instance, an independent landholder, Santiago Machego, arranged to have his son farm for Lawrence on shares, apparently so that he could obtain experience and training. JL May 6, 1870.

84 Leonard and Loomis, *Culture of a Contemporary Rural Community,* 70; Meinig, *Southwest,* chap. 5.

85 See, for example, a call for Protestant conversion of Catholics in *Minutes of the Forty-Seventh Session of the Colorado Annual Conference of the Methodist Episcopal Church Held in Pueblo* (Denver, 1909), 66.

work as in August, as the weather was fine and he should have taken advantage of it."[86]

This transition can be traced through the careers of the individuals examined here. In plazas where outside influences were few, the patrón system could function in its purest form. Lawrence maintained the intimate contact, economic bonds, and social responsibilities typical of the patrón, yet in his financial and political interests he looked beyond his locality and actively promoted regional development that would destroy conditions allowing the patrón system to exist. Vigil retained local relationships with the people of his home but by operating from Trinidad he reduced the bonds of close personal contact. Barela, often cited as the area's leading patrón, ironically cast off many characteristics of the system and entered the Anglo world of state politics and entrepreneurial development. In their adaptations, these men reflected the encroachment of Anglo society and culture transforming the life of southern Colorado.

Older inhabitants reacted to such change by retreating. Many Spanish-surname settlers withdrew to poorer lands south of the Conejos River.[87] Those who stayed kept to themselves, hoping to salvage the complex of relationships supporting their culture. In an atmosphere of discrimination, once frequent fiestas where Anglos and Mexican Americans joined hands became rare events worth special note.[88] By withdrawing and turning inward upon their communities, the older inhabitants of southern Colorado displayed a passive resistance that contrasted with the Anglos' passion to develop and dominate the region. As rural patrones lost their special claims on wealth and status, these isolated societies were gradually compressed into a single class of subsistence farmers, herders, and laborers. After the 1920s, a new influx of Mexican immigrants with little attachment to the land and a strong identification with their mother country further modified the society of southern Colorado. There remain only isolated plazas, reminders of thriving communities and a pattern of life that formed an important part of an earlier southwestern culture.

---

[86] Ira B. Gale to Vigil, Dec. 18, 1905, JUV.

[87] Carlson, "Rural Settlement Patterns in the San Luis Valley," 113–115, 119–120; William E. Pabor, *Colorado as an Agricultural State, Its Farms, Fields, and Garden Lands* (New York, 1883), 123–124.

[88] JL Jan. 2, 1896, Nov. 14, 1898, April 25, 1904.

Working on El Traque:
The Pacific Electric
Strike of 1903

Charles Wollenberg

The author is a member of the history department in Laney College.

DURING THE SPRING OF 1903, tracklayers worked night and day on the Los Angeles Main Street line of Henry E. Huntington's Pacific Electric railroad. The new downtown route had to be finished in time for the annual Los Angeles Fiesta on May 6 and 7. The P.E.'s electric cars were to be an important part of the festivities, not only carrying thousands of spectators into the downtown area, but also serving as elaborately decorated floats in the fiesta parade—a parade that was to be reviewed by President Theodore Roosevelt.

But on the morning of April 24, representatives of the Unión Federal Mexicanos (Mexican Federal Union) confronted company officials with a demand that wages of the largely Mexican track workers be raised from 17.5 cents per hour to 20 cents for day work, 30 cents for evenings, and 40 cents for Sundays.[1] Huntington, the railroad's president, was in San Francisco that morning, and the immediate company response was made by panicky subordinates. They agreed to all demands. But by afternoon, Huntington had countermanded that decision, and union representatives were informed that the morning's agreement was null and void. Angrily,

---

[1] *Los Angeles Record*, April 24, 1903; *Los Angeles Times*, April 25, 1903.

they called on track workers to leave the job, and it seems that all Mexicans, about 700 men, on the Main Street project did just that. By evening only sixty "Irishmen, Negroes and whites" remained at work.[2]

Thus began the Pacific Electric strike of 1903, one of the first major labor disputes between Mexican workers and Anglo employers in the United States. The strike occurred at a time when the first great wave of Mexican immigration was sweeping into the Southwest. Labor demands of American railroads were drawing thousands of Mexicans across the border, and *el traque*, as the immigrants called the railroad, was transporting Mexican workers throughout the country. Social, economic, and demographic patterns were being established which laid the groundwork for far larger migrations after World Wars I and II and for massive use of Mexican labor in southwestern agriculture, mining, and industry. The Pacific Electric strike of 1903 provides an insight into the beginnings of this great movement of people "north from Mexico." Moreover, the strike clearly indicates that even the earliest of these immigrants were willing to engage in militant, labor action.

Unfortunately, the pre-1910 migration of railroad workers has been largely ignored by students of Mexican-American history. Carey McWilliams devotes only two pages to the subject, while Matt S. Meier and Feliciano Rivera, and Leo Grebler and his co-authors give even briefer coverage.[3] The best sources remain Victor S. Clark's long monograph published in 1908 in the *Bulletin of the Bureau Labor* and Samuel Bryan's shorter 1912 article in *The Survey*.[4] Clark shared many of his contemporaries' unfavorable opinions about Mexicans, but his monograph gives detailed descriptions of employment practices and working conditions on *el traque*, surveys employers' attitudes about Mexicans, and includes some of the

---

[2] *Los Angeles Times*, April 25, 1903; *Los Angeles Record*, April 25, 1903.

[3] Carey McWilliams, *North from Mexico: The Spanish-Speaking People of the United States* (New York, Greenwood edition, 1968), 167–169; Leo Grebler *et al.*, *The Mexican-American People: The Nation's Second Largest Minority* (New York, 1970), 83, 89; Matt S. Meier and Feliciano Rivera, *The Chicanos: A History of Mexican Americans* (New York, 1972), 126.

[4] Victor S. Clark, "Mexican Labor in the United States," *Bulletin of the Bureau of Labor, No. 78* (Washington, 1908), 466–521; Samuel Bryan, "Mexican Immigrants in the United States," *The Survey*, XXVIII (1912), 726–730.

best Mexican immigration data we have from this period. Bryan summarized Clark's findings and provided a more sympathetic picture of the Mexican immigrants.

The 1903 strike itself is only briefly covered in Spencer Crump's *Ride the Big Red Cars* and Grace Heilman Stimson's *Rise of the Labor Movement in Los Angeles.*[5] Crump's book is a nostalgic history of the Pacific Electric, and while he grants some justice to the workers' cause, his general viewpoint is sympathetic to company management. Stimson provides detailed coverage of the many labor conflicts which plagued Los Angeles during this period and—in less than a page—covers the 1903 track workers' walkout as a minor offshoot of these larger disputes. Best information on the 1903 strike comes from contemporary newspapers, particularly the *Los Angeles Times,* which was vehemently anti-organized labor and thus supportive of the railroad's position, and the *Los Angeles Record,* equally vehement in its anti-Huntington editorial policy and thus sympathetic to the strikers.

The sharply opposing viewpoints of the *Times* and *Record* in part reflected controversies raging in Los Angeles over the role of Henry E. Huntington in southern California's economic development. In 1901 he sold the vast holdings of Southern Pacific stock inherited from his uncle, Collis P. Huntington, and organized a syndicate to build an electric rail line from Los Angeles to Long Beach.[6] The younger Huntington also began buying other street car lines in the vicinity and formed the Pacific Electric Company to serve as corporate structure for his new empire. By the end of the year, he had proclaimed his intention to "build an inter-urban system that will cover southern California."[7] Thus, Huntington became one of Los Angeles' major business leaders and employers. He also became a highly influential member of the Los Angeles Merchants and Manufacturers Association and the Citizens Alliance, employer groups determined to fight trade unions and maintain the "open shop" in southern California. "Unions," Huntington

[5] Spencer Crump, *Ride the Big Red Cars: How Trolleys Helped Build Southern California* (Los Angeles, 1962); Grace Heilman Stimson, *Rise of the Labor Movement in Los Angeles* (Berkeley and Los Angeles, 1955).

[6] McWilliams, *North from Mexico,* 169; Crump, *Ride the Big Red Cars,* 132.

[7] Crump, *Ride the Big Red Cars,* 133–134.

claimed, "are not organized for benefit, but for trouble . . . and they are harmful to the men themselves."[8]

In 1901 and 1902 he firmly put down attempts by Pacific Electric motormen and conductors to form a union, but in the spring of 1903 he faced still another challenge. Union organizers from San Francisco and the Los Angeles Council of Labor established a local of the Amalgamated Association of Street Car Employees to represent Pacific Electric carmen. At the same time, they offered to help Mexican workers form a separate union to represent construction laborers on the Huntington line.[9] Thus, on April 23, Lemuel Biddle, secretary of the Council of Labor, announced the establishment of the Unión Federal Mexicanos with A. N. Nieto as executive secretary. By the end of the month, the new organization claimed a membership of 900 track workers, a bank account of $600, and a small adobe headquarters in Los Angeles' "Sonoratown," the predominantly Mexican neighborhood north of the Central Plaza.[10]

The Unión Federal was probably the first union of Mexican track workers in the United States. At the time the Unión was formed, Mexicans were coming to dominate track work on the railroads of the West and Southwest. In the 1860s, the back-breaking job of building the first transcontinental was largely accomplished by Chinese and Irish. Italians, Greeks, and Japanese entered the field in later years, but by the end of the nineteenth century, southwestern lines were showing preference for Mexicans over other nationalities. Victor Clark interviewed several employers in 1907 and reported that "there was not a single instance in which the men in actual touch with railroad labor did not give the Mexican preference over either Japanese or Greeks." A Texas railroad man said he was substituting Mexicans for "Italians who are disorderly. . . . [The Mexicans] suit us better than any other immigrant labor."[11]

Clark's respondents claimed Mexicans were more "docile" than other nationalities, particularly the Japanese. Employers believed that Mexicans were "patient[,] usually orderly in camp, fairly in-

---

[8] *Ibid.*, 128; Stimson, *Rise of the Labor Movement*, 258.

[9] Stimson, *Rise of the Labor Movement*, 266; Crump, *Ride the Big Red Cars*, 128, 133.

[10] Stimson, *Rise of the Labor Movement*, 267; *Los Angeles Times*, April 27, 1903; *Los Angeles Record*, April 28, 1903.

[11] Clark, "Mexican Labor," 477–478.

telligent under competent supervision and cheap." If Mexicans were "more active and ambitious," they would be "less tractable and cost more."[12] On the other hand, "every Japanese gang is a trade union." "When you have occasion to discharge one Japanese, all would quit. . . . But if a Mexican proves a poor or undesirable workman, you can let him go without breaking up the entire gang." Somewhat contradictorily, employers also reported that Mexicans were considered "very tenacious of their rights" and would quit "if they believe they are being cheated."[13]

Cultural stereotypes aside, Clark probably was correct when he concluded that the Mexican's "strongest point" with employers was "his willingness to work for a low wage."[14] Most Mexican rail workers received from $1.00 to $1.25 for a ten-hour day, while other nationalities often were paid up to $1.75 for similar work. In parts of southern California, the Southern Pacific paid different wages for different nationalities: $1.60 for Greeks, $1.45 for Japanese, and $1.25 for Mexicans, yet foremen admitted that all groups did about the same work at about the same level of efficiency.[15] However, Huntington initially paid higher wages than other employers to attract workers during early stages of heavy construction on the Pacific Electric. In 1901 P.E. offered Mexican laborers $1.85 per day, but by the middle of the decade, as construction slowed, P.E. wages fell to about the same level as those of southern California steam lines.[16]

But even the $1.00 to $1.25 wage was approximately double what a Mexican laborer could earn for similar work in his own country.[17] For many of the workers, the migration to the United States was simply an extension of migrations within Mexico itself. President Porfirio Díaz had imposed domestic order in Mexico during the late nineteenth century, and this helped stimulate rapid economic development in northern Mexico. Construction of the Mexican Central and Mexican National railroads, as well as the opening of new mines and agricultural enterprises, created a great demand for

---

12 *Ibid.*, 496.
13 *Ibid.*, 478, 499.
14 *Ibid.*, 496.
15 Bryan, "Mexican Immigrants," 728; Clark, "Mexican Labor," 478–479.
16 Crump, *Ride the Big Red Cars*, 133–134.
17 Clark, "Mexican Labor," 470.

labor in the sparsely-settled north. Once attracted from the villages of southern and central Mexico, men were willing to move even further north, even across the border, in search of higher wages. By 1907 northern Mexican railroads were having difficulty keeping section gangs at full strength. The Mexican National claimed that virtually an entire work crew of 1500 men had moved into Texas during the year.[18]

Most Mexicans who crossed the border intended to stay in the United States only a few months. Train fare to the border from central Mexican states such as Jalisco or Guanajuato, which were among the leading suppliers of immigrants, was about $10 to $15 (U.S. dollars). A Mexican peasant could raise this by selling farm animals or borrowing from local moneylenders. The peasant's family might cultivate his fields while he was away, thus maintaining the family's traditional source of income which could be supplemented by anything the worker might send or bring back from the north.[19] By the end of the decade, increasing numbers of men were crossing the border with families in tow, probably a sign that they were intending to stay in the United States. However, in 1908 Clark still believed that about two-thirds of the workers were temporary migrants.[20]

El Paso, the northern railhead of the Mexican Central, was the largest distribution point for Mexican railroad labor in the United States, including labor on the Pacific Electric. Most recruitment was done at El Paso by private employment agencies on contract with the railroads. Agencies rarely recruited in Mexico, but met immigrants at the border with offers of immediate jobs. The worker was not charged for this service; agencies usually received a dollar per man delivered from the railroad and were allowed to operate profitable commissaries where workers bought meals and merchandise on credit at prices from five to ten percent above normal market levels. (Debts to the commissary were usually deducted from paychecks.)[21]

The largest employers of Mexican immigrants naturally were railroads operating in the West and Southwest, not only the Pacific Electric, but lines such as the Southern Pacific and Santa Fe. Never-

---

18 *Ibid.*, 468–470; Bryan, "Mexican Immigrants," 727.
19 Clark, "Mexican Labor," 472–473.
20 *Ibid.*, 521.
21 Bryan, "Mexican Immigrants," 728; Clark, "Mexican Labor," 474–476.

theless, substantial numbers of Mexicans could be found repairing track as far north as the Great Lakes. Labor on all lines which employed Mexicans was ethnically stratified. Only Anglos served as carmen (engineers, motormen, conductors, and so forth), while Mexicans were employed almost exclusively on track work (construction crews building new lines or "extra" and "section" gangs maintaining existing lines).[22] Thus, when the Pacific Electric strike broke out in 1903, Mexican track workers and Anglo carmen were in separate unions, reflecting the ethnic and occupational separation that existed on the P.E.

Most railroads had great difficulty in keeping Mexicans on the job, for *el traque* was considered a sure but not attractive source of employment. One worker, interviewed by Manuel Gamio in the 1920s, claimed that he had worked for the railroad "because there wasn't anything else and one always needs money. One has to work or starve."[23] A common pattern was for a recent arrival from Mexico to work on *el traque* until he found something else less grueling or more lucrative. Desertions became so common that trains transporting men to new work sites were often sealed. The Southern Pacific and Santa Fe offered free passage back to Mexico for those who remained on the job for a given length of time (one year for S.P., six months for Santa Fe), but only about half the workers stayed long enough to take advantage of such offers.[24]

However, Henry E. Huntington did not have to resort to these practices as long as he paid wages higher than those of his steam competitors. Pacific Electric attracted deserters from other lines rather than suffering desertions from its own job sites. A jovial P.E. official boasted that "Southern Pacific brings 155 Mexicans in and we hire 156 of them."[25] Such statements reflected the intense competition for labor among railroads; by 1908 an immigrant could arrive at the border "practically without funds, but with the moral certainty of securing immediate employment."[26] In that year El Paso agencies were placing more than 2,000 railroad workers per

22 Bryan, "Mexican Immigrants," 728–729.

23 Manuel Gamio, *The Mexican Immigrant: His Life Story* (Chicago, 1931), 16, 92–93, 97.

24 Clark, "Mexican Labor," 472, 479; Bryan, "Mexican Immigrants," 729.

25 Crump, *Ride the Big Red Cars,* 133–134.

26 Clark, "Mexican Labor," 475.

month, and labor contractors estimated that 60,000 to 100,000 Mexicans were crossing the border annually.[27] Some of these men found work in agriculture, mining, and urban construction, but Samuel Bryan claimed that "most Mexicans have at one time or another been employed as railroad laborers," and Victor Clark believed that, "with the possible exception of agriculture during certain seasons, more Mexicans are employed as railroad laborers than at any other occupation. It is from this occupation that they drift into other lines of work."[28]

Confident of his ability to attract such workers, Huntington refused to deal with the Unión Federal during the 1903 strike. As a Pacific Electric spokesman told the *Los Angeles Times*, "Mr. Huntington proposes to run his own affairs and can in no matter accept union dictation."[29] The *Times* believed that "agitators" were behind the strike. They had "deluded the poor ignorant peons employed in laying track on the local Huntington roads into forming a 'union'—stupid fellows, these peons, who don't know what a union is. . . ."[30] A company spokesman assured the newspaper that money was not the issue. Huntington would have met the workers' wage demand had it not been for "union agitators." The Main Street line would be finished by fiesta time if the company had to pay five dollars per day, but under no circumstances would strikers be rehired.[31]

The railroad did, in fact, raise wages on the Main Street line to 22¢ per hour, two cents above the day wages demanded by the union. Mexican workers from other Huntington lines were brought in, and Japanese, Negro, and white laborers were recruited in Los Angeles. By April 27 full crews again were working on the project.[32] The next day the strikers, led by a woman mystic and healer who was well-known to the Los Angeles Mexicans as "Santa Teresa," staged a procession along the job site. The demonstration briefly disrupted work, and more than fifty of the newly-recruited laborers laid down their tools and joined the strike.[33]

---

27 Bryan, "Mexican Immigrants," 727–728; Clark, "Mexican Labor," 466.
28 Clark, "Mexican Labor," 475, 477; Bryan, "Mexican Immigrants," 728.
29 *Los Angeles Times*, April 25, 1903.
30 *Ibid.*
31 *Ibid.*
32 *Ibid.*, April 27, 1903.
33 *Los Angeles Record*, April 28, 1903.

Meanwhile, the union claimed it had obtained support from American Federation of Labor president, Samuel Gompers, and San Francisco Union Labor Party mayor, Eugene Schmitz. Unions affiliated with the Los Angeles Council of Labor and the local chapter of the Socialist party made financial contributions to the Mexican workers' cause. The *Los Angeles Socialist* reported that "lady comrades Miss Wilkins and Mrs. McLeod . . . were cheering and ministering to the families of the brave men who may not talk the English language."[34]

Union strategy apparently was to keep large numbers of Mexican track workers off the Main Street job until April 29 when Anglo carmen affiliated with the Amalgamated Association of Street Car Employees planned a walkout that was supposed to shut down the entire Huntington system. At 7:30 P.M. conductors and motormen were to stop their cars and leave them wherever they happened to be. Huntington warned that any man leaving his post would immediately be fired, and the railroad had police and emergency crews on hand to deal with the planned walkout.[35] When the appointed hour came, only twelve carmen out of a total of 764 on duty left their posts; service continued almost without interruption. A disgusted San Francisco union organizer said it was a case of "cold feet"; "many of the boys, at the last moment, refused to walk out."[36]

The April 29 fiasco not only doomed the attempt to organize motormen and conductors, it also killed the track workers' strike. While the Unión Federal showed far greater ability to keep workers off the job than the Amalgamated, Huntington had been able to find more than enough replacements for strikers. Union spokesman Nieto still expressed confidence, but even the anti-Huntington *Los Angeles Record* noted that the idle workers were "becoming restless."[37] In the beginning of June, the *Record* reported that most strikers had "drifted away" or "secured other employment." Meanwhile, the fiesta had been a great success. The Main Street line was completed with time to spare, Huntington's decorated trolley cars

---

34 *Los Angeles Socialist*, May 2, 1903; *Los Angeles Record*, April 28, 1903.

35 *Los Angeles Times*, April 30, 1903; *Los Angeles Record*, April 29 and 30, 1903.

36 *Los Angeles Record*, April 30, 1903.

37 *Ibid.*, May 8, 1903. Even during the strike, the *Times* claimed that there was dissension among the workers and that the union treasury had been pilfered. *Los Angeles Times*, April 25 and 27, 1903.

were the highpoint of the show, and President Roosevelt had a fine time.[38]

The failure of the 1903 strike did not end conflict between Henry Huntington and the men of *el traque*. In 1904 a temporarily-revived Unión Federal protested the Pacific Electric's decision to reduce track workers' wages from $1.75 to $1.00 per day. The company explained that the reduction simply reflected rent owed by workers for housing supplied by the railroad, but, if this were true, the men were paying about double the normal rent for such housing.[39] Most workers lived in barrack-like "housecourts," divided into several one- or two-room apartments. Such an apartment might be home for eight to ten people.[40] Dr. J. Powers of the Los Angeles County Health Department described some of the railroad housing as "a menace to public health and a disgrace to civilized communities." "Conditions around the houses," he claimed, "would not be tolerable in a stable." The *Record* reported that "sanitation was a jest. Decency was impossible."[41] Nevertheless, the company made the wage reductions stick, and a decade later conditions in the housecourts showed little improvement.[42] In 1910 Mexican workers again struck Pacific Electric for higher wages; again Huntington successfully broke the strike.[43] But that was to be his last battle with the men of *el traque*. Within a year, he had sold Pacific Electric to the Southern Pacific.

After 1910, far more Mexicans crossed the border to follow the harvests than to work on the railroads of the Southwest. Irrigated agriculture boomed, while most southwestern rail construction had been completed. It is true that in 1926 the six largest southwestern railroads still employed more than 50,000 Mexicans at peak periods, and, on those lines, Mexicans comprised more than seventy-five percent of extra gang and section gang personnel.[44] The 1930 census

---

38 *Los Angeles Record*, May 7 and 8, June 6, 1903.

39 Stimson, *Rise of the Labor Movement*, 267; Crump, *Ride the Big Red Cars*, 134; *Los Angeles Record*, April 6 and 7, 1904; William McEuen, "A Survey of the Mexicans in Los Angeles" (M.A. thesis, University of Southern California, 1914), 32.

40 Bryan, "Mexican Immigrants," 730; Clark, "Mexican Labor," 507–508; McEuen, "Survey of Mexicans," 39–45.

41 *Los Angeles Record*, April 6, 1904.

42 McEuen, "Survey of Mexicans," 39–45.

43 *Los Angeles Times*, March 2, 1910; Stimson, *Rise of the Labor Movement*, 336.

44 Governor C. C. Young's Mexican Fact-Finding Committee, *Mexicans In California* (San Francisco, 1930), 91.

listed 70,000 Mexicans employed in "transportation and communication," and, after Pearl Harbor, railroads were able to import workers under the provisions of the bracero program. By 1944 more than 40,000 railroad braceros were working in the United States.[45] But these figures were dwarfed by the numbers of Mexicans working in southwestern agriculture and industry.

Nevertheless, the pre-1910 migration of Mexican track workers had left its mark on the Southwest. Unfortunately, official United States figures for Mexican immigration during the period were notoriously inaccurate, but the U.S. census returns showed a spectacular growth of Mexican-born residents between 1900 and 1910, from 103,393 to 221,915. Even these totals greatly understated the scope of migration, since most railroad workers were highly transient and not likely to be encountered by census takers.[46] For Los Angeles, the 1910 census reported a Mexican-born population of 8,917, but local scholars and public officials put the actual total at not less than 20,000, a good portion of which had worked for Pacific Electric at one time or another.[47] After World War I, the Los Angeles housecourts and labor camps of pre-1910 days became nuclei of sprawling urban *barrios*; the city was becoming the largest Mexican community in the United States and one of the largest in the world.

But the men who crossed the border to work on *el traque* during the first decade of the twentieth century not only were forerunners of a great migration, they also began a seventy year heritage of class and ethnic struggle. The 1903 Pacific Electric strike clearly is part of that heritage, and further research is needed to determine if there were other strikes of Mexican workers on other southwestern railroads. Perhaps the 1903 walkout was unique because Pacific Electric, unlike other southwestern lines, was primarily an urban enterprise. Track workers in the Los Angeles area were in contact with a fairly large and well-developed Mexican community. Los

45 Ernesto Galarza, *Merchants of Labor: The Mexican Bracero Story* (San Jose, 1964), 53–55; McWilliams, *North from Mexico*, 168. After World War II, railroad braceros, unlike those in agriculture, were banned from further employment in the United States.

46 Grebler *et al.*, *Mexican-American People*, 64; Manuel Gamio, *Mexican Immigration to the United States* (Chicago, 1930), 2.

47 McEuen, "Survey of Mexicans," 4.

Angeles also had an active Council of Labor, and the cooperation between that body and the Unión Federal during the 1903 strike should be studied in comparison with the later hostility the Council showed toward Mexican unions. But even without further research and elaboration the story of the Pacific Electric strike stands as an historical contradiction to generalizations about the "passivity" and "tractability" of Mexican labor. The men who walked off the Main Street job, migrants who had crossed the Rio Grande during the earliest years of this century, clearly had a sense of grievance, a willingness to engage in collective action, and an ability to carry out such action. The 1903 Pacific Electric strike was a precursor of the struggles currently being waged in the fields and barrios of the Southwest.

Stimulus to Repatriation: The 1931 Federal Deportation Drive and the Los Angeles Mexican Community

Abraham Hoffman

The author is a member of the history department in the University of Oaklahoma.

During the early years of the Great Depression, thousands of Mexican aliens and their families left the United States and went "back to their homeland." Although the departure of Mexican immigrants has been mentioned by a few writers, most notably Carey McWilliams, the movement has never been treated in detail.[1] Inquiry into the repatriation movement reveals that the peak period during which destitute Mexican aliens returned to Mexico was preceded by a federal deportation drive centered on the Los Angeles area. In order to understand the context in which this drive took place, it should be noted that much of the impetus for the move-

---

[1] Carey McWilliams has described the departures, with emphasis on Los Angeles, in *North from Mexico: the Spanish-Speaking People of the United States* (Philadelphia and New York, 1949), 193; the book has recently been reprinted, but his work is badly in need of revision. See also McWilliams' *Factories in the Field: the Story of Migratory Farm Labor in California* (Boston, 1939), 129; *Southern California Country: An Island on the Land* (New York, 1946), 315–317; "Getting Rid of the Mexican," *American Mercury*, XXVIII (March 1933), 322–324; and "A Man, a Place, and a Time," *American West*, VII (May 1970), 7. McWilliams, who was (and still is) a provocative writer, has too often been taken as definitive. Most writers who considered the repatriation movement did so when it took place, or not long afterward, and their work is out of date. Important articles by Robert N. McLean include "Goodbye, Vicente!" *Survey*, LXVI (May 1, 1931), 182–183; "Hard Times Oust the Mexican,"

109

ment of Mexicans out of the country came from policies inaugurated on the national level. Believing that aliens were holding down jobs that could have been held by native-born Americans, President Herbert Hoover had endorsed a strenuous effort to curtail both legal and illegal alien entries and approved the vigorous prosecution of aliens living illegally in the United States. As a result of these policies, 1931 became a year filled with events often unrelated to the goal ofreducing unemployment. Misinformation on legal procedures, "voluntary" deportation, and contradictory pronouncements by officials created a controversy which aroused international attention.[2]

Much of the problem resulted from Hoover's appointment of William N. Doak as Secretary of Labor to replace James J. Davis, who had been elected to the Senate. Doak promised to find a way to solve the national unemployment problem. Soon after taking office on December 9, 1930, the new Labor Secretary proclaimed his solution. One way to provide work for unemployed Americans, he announced, was to oust aliens holding jobs. There were 400,000 aliens who were illegal residents in the United States, asserted Doak, and, under current immigration laws, 100,000 were deportable. Following upon the creation of the United States Border Patrol in 1925 and the high rejection rate of visa applications from prospective immigrants in 1928 and afterward, Doak's announcement

---

Mexican Life, VII (Sept. 1931), 19–21; and "The Mexican Return," *Nation,* CXXXV (Aug. 24, 1932), 165–166. Emory S. Bogardus, among his many writings on Mexicans in the United States, discussed repatriation in "Mexican Repatriates," *Sociology and Social Research,* XVIII (1933), 169–176; and *The Mexican in the United States* (Los Angeles, 1934), chap. 13. Repatriation was also discussed in Manuel Gamio, *Mexican Immigration to the United States: A Study of Human Migration and Adjustment* (Chicago, 1930), 233–241. See also Paul S. Taylor, "Mexican Labor in the United States: Migration Statistics, IV," *University of California Publications in Economics,* XII (1934), 23–49; and Taylor, *A Spanish-Mexican Peasant Community: Arandas in Jalisco, Mexico* (Berkeley, 1933), 55–67.

It should be noted that the few recent books which mention repatriation base their accounts on one or more of the above authors and that no recent studies in depth have been done on the repatriation movement. The deportation campaign, which is the subject of this article, has received even less notice than the repatriation movement, of which it was a part. On the distinctions between deportation and repatriation in Los Angeles, see Abraham Hoffman, "The Repatriation of Mexican Nationals from the United States During the Great Depression" (Ph.D. dissertation, University of California, Los Angeles, 1970), chaps. 3–5, and Appendix A.

2 Irving Bernstein, *The Lean Years: A History of the American Worker, 1920–1933* (Boston, 1960), 305–306; National Commission on Law Observance and Enforcement, "Report on the Enforcement of the Deportation Laws of the United States," *Report No. 5* (May 27, 1931), *passim.*

launched a campaign which one writer called a "gladiatorial spectacle." More aliens left the United States in the first nine months of 1931 than entered it. Doak's immigration agents raided both public and private places seeking aliens who were deportable, and they did so in a search which extended from New York to Los Angeles.[3]

Doak's campaign made no effort to single out any specific ethnic group, but most of those affected turned out to be Mexicans living in southern California, home for half the state's 368,000 Mexicans.[4] A sequence of events occurred in Los Angeles that resulted in a concentration of effort by the Department of Labor to root out deportable aliens living in that area. The fears aroused by the activities of the federal agents there contributed to a mass exodus of thousands of men, women, and children.

At the root of the deportation drive lay the depression itself. With unemployment high in Los Angeles, concerned civic officials and business leaders had tried to help solve the problem. In line with President Hoover's Emergency Committee for Employment (PECE), the Los Angeles city and county governments formed local citizens' relief committees. On Christmas Eve of 1930, Charles P. Visel was named coordinator of the city committee; his plan "was to contact all government, industrial and private sources of labor with a view toward creation of employment." Committee members included Mayor John C. Porter, County Supervisor Frank L. Shaw, *Los Angeles Times* publisher Harry Chandler, Los Angeles Chamber of Commerce President John C. Austin, and various city officials and business executives.[5] The county committee was to handle all

---

[3] Roger W. Babson, *Washington and the Depression: Including the Career of W. N. Doak* (New York, 1932), 92–93; Bernstein, *Lean Years,* 334; Gardner Jackson, "Doak the Deportation Chief," *Nation,* CXXXII (March 18, 1931), 295–296; *New York Times,* Jan. 6, 1931; Robert S. Allen, "One of Mr. Hoover's Friends," *American Mercury,* XXV (Jan. 1932), 58.

[4] The heaviest concentration of Mexicans in the United States in 1930 was in Los Angeles County, where 167,024 were counted in the 1930 census. Neighboring San Bernardino County had 24,365 Mexicans. Texas had the greatest number (over 683,000), but with lesser urban concentration. Some 98,901 Mexicans lived in Bexar County, with 82,373 within the city limits of San Antonio. Arizona's Maricopa County (county seat of Phoenix) had 32,494 Mexicans. Within the city limits of Los Angeles alone there lived 97,116 Mexicans. U.S. Bureau of the Census, *Fifteenth Census of the United States 1930: Population* (Washington, 1933), III, part 1, pp. 157, 233, 266, part 2, pp. 1014–1015.

[5] Los Angeles *Illustrated Daily News,* Dec. 25, 1930; Erving P. Hayes, *Activities of the President's Emergency Committee for Employment, 1930–1931* (Concord, 1936), 103–107, *passim.*

unemployed people not residents of the city of Los Angeles, but the two committees planned to work together.[6]

Visel soon placed a curious interpretation on his responsibilities. On January 6, 1931, he sent a telegram to Colonel Arthur M. Woods, who had been appointed by Hoover as national coordinator of PECE. Visel had learned of Doak's declaration about the 400,000 illegal aliens, and, by a calculation known only to himself, he estimated that five percent, or between 20,000 to 25,000 of them, could be found in southern California. The local immigration office lacked the personnel for a program of mass arrest and deportation, but Visel indicated that the police and sheriff's offices might lend assistance if asked to do so. "You advise please as to method of getting rid. . . . We need their jobs for needy citizens," read the telegram.[7]

Visel received a reply from Woods on January 8, in which the national coordinator asked him to contact Secretary Doak, and to state definitely how far the local law enforcement authorities would go in cooperating with the federal immigration officials. "There is every willingness at this end of the line," stated Woods, "to act thoroughly and promptly."[8] Visel promptly wired Doak and urged the Labor Secretary to send agents from several other cities to create a "psychological gesture." It was not Visel's intention to press the Bureau of Immigration into actually conducting an indefinite number of deportation hearings, but rather to establish an environment hostile enough to alarm aliens. "This apparent activity," Visel's telegram promised Doak, "will have tendency to scare many thousand alien deportables out of this district which is the result desired." Doak responded quickly to Visel's telegram and thanked him for his efforts.[9]

---

6 Los Angeles *Illustrated Daily News*, Dec. 27, 1930. The existence of two committees was due to Mayor Porter's unhappiness in being edged out by Shaw for the chairmanship of the county committee.

7 Telegram from Woods to Visel, Jan. 6, 1931, George P. Clements Papers, Department of Special Collections, University of California, Los Angeles. All citations from the Clements Papers are from material in Bundle 15, Box 80. The National Archives, Record Group 73 (PECE Papers), also has copies of the telegrams. See entry 3, 040, U–Z, PECE Papers. (National Archives and Record Group cited hereafter as NA RG.) Because of marginal notations, both sources are cited.

8 Woods to Visel, Jan. 8, 1931, Clements Papers; and NA RG 73, entry 3, 040, U–Z, PECE Papers.

9 Telegram from Visel to Doak, Jan. 11, 1931; and Doak to Visel, Jan. 12, 1931, Clements Papers; and NA RG 73, entry 3, 040, U–Z, PECE Papers.

The plan of Coordinator Visel to scare aliens into leaving southern California was built along simple lines. First, there would be publicity releases announcing the deportation campaign and stressing that help would be given the local immigration office from adjoining districts. Then a few arrests would be made, "with all publicity possible and pictures." Both police and deputy sheriffs would assist. It was hoped that some aliens would be frightened into leaving and others would steer clear of Los Angeles. Visel interviewed Walter E. Carr, the district's immigration director, for his thoughts on the plan. Visel afterward quoted him as saying that much time would be saved if "a large number of these aliens, actuated by guilty self-consciousness, would move south and over the line of their own accord, particularly if stimulated by a few arrests under the Deportation Act." It was also clearly understood before the campaign began that the primary targets were the Mexican aliens living in southern California.[10]

The Mexican colony in southern California at this time constituted the largest minority group in the area, far outnumbering Orientals or aliens from European countries. Many Mexicans who had entered the United States illegally—in the sense that they had not bothered to line up for a visa in the years of lax enforcement by the immigration service, or had "bootlegged" themselves across in order to avoid paying the federal head tax or visa fees—and who had lived for years in southern California and elsewhere, were made suddenly aware of their vulnerability. Life during the depression was already difficult for Mexican nationals. Both the Los Angeles City Council and the County Board of Supervisors had indicated support for state legislation barring aliens from employment on public works projects.[11] Crimes involving people with Spanish surnames made headlines; during the week that Visel's plans went into operation, two separate felony cases involving Mexicans were also being followed daily.[12]

---

10 Visel to Woods, Jan. 19, 1931; see also untitled memorandum of Jan. 24, 1931, Clements Papers. Cf. NA RG 73, entry 3, 040, PECE Papers. For Carr's denial of Visel's views, see Carr to Commissioner General of Immigration Harry Hull, June 17, 1931, NA RG 85, file 55739/674.

11 *Los Angeles Record*, Nov. 24 and 25, Dec. 17, 1930, April 17, 1931; *Los Angeles Evening Express*, April 17, 1931; *Los Angeles Times*, Jan. 13, 1931.

12 See *Los Angeles Times*, Jan. 25, 1931; *Los Angeles Examiner*, Jan. 26, 1931; and succeeding issues for that week.

Visel submitted his plans for publicity to Colonel Woods, who committed the error of giving the publicity release a careless reading. He failed to consider how Visel's words might be interpreted in a city that, except for Mexico City, contained within its population the largest number of Mexican nationals. Instead, he informed Doak of Visel's intentions, and Doak authorized the sending of a special officer and several agents to Los Angeles to investigate the presence of illegal aliens.[13]

Visel's publicity release was published in the Los Angeles newspapers on Monday, January 26, 1931, with additional items in the days following. Each newspaper printed the text as it saw fit, so that while one newspaper printed sections of it verbatim, another summarized and paraphrased. Certain embellishments were added: "Aliens who are deportable will save themselves trouble and expense," suggested the *Illustrated Daily News*, "by arranging their departure at once." The *Los Angeles Examiner* announced, "Deportable aliens include Mexicans, Japanese, Chinese, and others," without going into any qualifying details. The impending arrival of the special agents from Washington, D.C., and other immigration districts was made known, the word being given by Visel to the newspapers.[14]

La Opinion, the leading Spanish-language newspaper in Los Angeles, published an extensive article on Thursday, January 29. With a major headline spread across page one, the newspaper quoted from Visel's release and from the versions of it given by the *Los Angeles Times* and *Illustrated Daily News*. *La Opinion*'s article pointedly stressed that the deportation campaign was aimed primarily at those of Mexican nationality.[15]

By the end of the week, it became apparent that the announcements of an impending deportation campaign were attracting the attention of more than just the readership of Los Angeles newspapers. The Mexican government, observing the movement of re-

---

13 Telegram from Woods to Visel, and attached memorandum, Jan. 23, 1931, NA RG 73, entry 3, 040, PECE Papers. There is nothing to indicate that Doak ever saw the publicity release.

14 See Los Angeles *Illustrated Daily News, Los Angeles Examiner,* and *Los Angeles Times,* Jan. 26, 1931; *Los Angeles Evening Express,* Jan. 28, 1931; *Los Angeles Times,* Jan. 29, 1931; and Los Angeles *Illustrated Daily News,* Jan. 30, 1931.

15 Los Angeles *La Opinion,* Jan. 29, 1931.

patriates southward from the United States for some time,[16] received word of the announcements in Los Angeles. Its Foreign Relations Department contacted Rafael de la Colina, the Mexican consul in Los Angeles, and instructed him to send a report describing the possibility of a large number of Mexicans resident in Los Angeles being deported.[17] The consul had been working with Los Angeles authorities on the idea of repatriating destitute Mexicans, and also assisting the Mexican community itself in raising donations for that purpose. But a plan to deport de la Colina's compatriots in great numbers was something else again. Contacting the Los Angeles Chamber of Commerce's George P. Clements, an advocate of Mexican labor in the United States, de la Colina asked him to urge all persons involved in the publicity to restate and clarify their intentions in the newspapers.[18]

The involvement of the Los Angeles Chamber of Commerce in the deportation campaign came from that organization's relief efforts in the latter months of 1930. Visel had been keeping the chamber informed of his relief plans, including the deportation-scare idea. As early as January 8 Arthur G. Arnoll, the chamber's general manager, had cautioned Visel to keep his publicity "from upsetting the whole Mexican population by wholesale raids which are misunderstood by the Mexican," and which might also disturb the communities that served California's agricultural labor needs.[19] Therefore, when Clements left the office of the Mexican consul, his intentions were to make Visel aware that the scare campaign was ill-advised in its application to an entire ethnic community.

Either Visel recognized the misinterpretations possible in his publicity or else he was made aware of its potential by Clements; at any rate, Visel agreed to accompany Clements to the office of District Director Carr. It was then decided that a statement denying the intention of a deportation campaign which focused on Mexican

16 Report of Consul General Robert Frazer to State Department, Jan. 28, 1931, NA RG 59, file 812.5511/107. The movement of *repatriados* is frequently mentioned in articles in the Los Angeles *La Opinion*; see also Taylor, "Mexican Labor in U.S.: Migration Statistics, IV," 24.

17 *Los Angeles Evening Express,* Jan. 30, 1931, and *Los Angeles Times,* Jan. 31, 1931; memo from Clements to A. G. Arnoll, Jan. 31, 1931, Clements Papers.

18 Memo from Clements to Arnoll, Jan. 31, 1931, Clements Papers; Los Angeles *La Opinion,* Jan. 30, 1931.

19 Arnoll to Visel, Jan. 8, 1931, Clements Papers.

aliens should be published as quickly as possible. Carr hastily drafted such a statement and sent it to the local newspapers. But the manner in which the press treated the statement failed to clarify the intentions of the immigration service; if anything, the bureau's motives were misinterpreted all the more. The *Evening Herald* quoted Carr's statement at length, the *Evening Express* somewhat less so, while the *Times* and the *Illustrated Daily News* simply ran brief summaries. The *Examiner* failed to publish anything. *La Opinion* again ran a major front-page article, assuring its readers that the intention of the federal government was to prosecute aliens with criminal records. This interpretation of the deportation drive was the one given by Carr to all the newspapers. When the actual campaign began, however, it proceeded on plans rather divergent from the direction promised by Carr.[20]

On the morning of the following day, January 31, Supervisor W. F. Watkins of the Bureau of Immigration arrived in Los Angeles, largely unaware of the publicity which had preceded him. In a meeting with Visel, Chief of Police Roy E. Steckel, and Sheriff William I. Traeger, Watkins soon learned that Visel had no basis for his assertion that 20,000 deportable aliens were in the Los Angeles area. The plan to scare Mexicans out of the area without the bother of formal deportation hearings was grounded in vagueness and lacked specific evidence. Watkins recognized the fallacy behind the scheme immediately. "The success of such idea is, of course, open to question," said Watkins, "as doubtless many aliens who have wilfully and knowingly entered the United States in violation of law would not choose to so easily forfeit their improperly acquired privileges here, and would more likely move further from the border rather than toward it, as a result of these deportation activities."[21]

Watkins was also unhappy over the publicity being given to the arrival of himself, his agents, and the proposed drive on aliens. During the first few days of February he and his men apprehended thirty-five aliens, his progress being followed closely by the Los

---

20 Clements' meeting with Visel and Carr is described in Clements' memo to Arnoll, Jan. 31, 1931, *ibid*. For the newspaper accounts, see *Los Angeles Evening Herald* and *Los Angeles Evening Express*, Jan. 30, 1931; *Los Angeles Times*, Los Angeles *Illustrated Daily News*, and Los Angeles *La Opinion*, Jan. 31, 1931.

21 Watkins to Assistant Secretary of Labor R. C. White, Feb. 8, 1931, NA RG 85, file 55739/674. Watkins brought eighteen agents with him to Los Angeles.

Angeles newspapers. In addition, Police Chief Steckel and Sheriff Traeger proved less than enthusiastic about lending their support.[22]

At this point Supervisor Watkins committed an error: he decided to go through with a roundup of aliens despite his learning that misrepresentations had been made to the Department of Labor and that the semi-secret nature of the work had been seriously compromised by all the publicity. Watkins had already run into the situation where some suspected aliens stopped by his men presented head tax receipts or some other proof of entry, as if they had anticipated examination. He did not know that Visel had announced that aliens should do this before the supervisor arrived.[23] Though Watkins branded the idea of picking up large numbers of contraband aliens at will as a "fantasy" of Los Angeles officials, his decision to stop and investigate large numbers of people in the hopes of capturing a few deportable aliens served to aggravate an already tense situation. Unaware of the propensity of the Los Angeles press to write headlines before all the facts were in, and uninformed on particular problems of ethnic minorities in Los Angeles, Watkins nonetheless decided to press the investigation. In doing so he showed a suprising lack of awareness as to why Mexicans had crossed the border, the length of time they had been crossing it, and the individual problems so many of them had encountered.[24]

If Watkins thought that Visel had been discouraged by the more realistic attitude presented by the immigration agents, the impression would have been a mistaken one. Visel was pleased at the arrival of the outside inspectors, for Watkins and his men proceeded to do just what Visel's plans had called for. Though at this point Watkins was just beginning his investigations, Visel was enthusiastic. "There is an aggressive campaign under way right now with, so far, gratifying results," he announced.[25]

The month of February saw a concerted drive on aliens in the Los Angeles area and its suburbs. Considering Carr's previous announcements that no ethnic group was being singled out and that only aliens with criminal records were the primary interest of the

---

22 *Ibid.*; Los Angeles *La Opinion*, Feb. 6, 7, 10, and 14, 1931; *Los Angeles Examiner*, Feb. 3, 1931.

23 *Los Angeles Times*, Jan. 29, 1931.

24 Watkins to White, Feb. 8, 1931, NA RG 85, file 55739/674.

25 Visel to Woods, Feb. 3, 1931, NA RG 73, entry 3, 040, PECE Papers.

Bureau of Immigration, the aliens questioned, arrested, or detained in the drive could only have made the Mexican community wary of official statements. A raid in the El Monte area on February 13 necessitated questioning 300 people, out of which thirteen were arrested. Twelve of the thirteen were Mexicans with no criminal records, their only offense being a failure to prove legal entry.[26]

Watkins doggedly pursued the search for deportable aliens. After several forays into East Los Angeles, the agents found the streets deserted, with local merchants complaining that the investigations were bad for business. In the rural sections of the county surveyed by Watkins' men, whole families disappeared from sight. Watkins also began to appreciate the extent of southern California's residential sprawl. He observed that, according to the 1930 census, the Belvedere section might hold as many as 60,000 Mexicans.[27]

Watkins had more direct success in his searches when he assigned several inspectors to check for possible aliens held in jail for other crimes. Nineteen such aliens found out of 200 prisoners questioned. In the first three weeks of February, the immigration agents checked and questioned several thousand people at various places throughout the county. By February 21, some 225 aliens subject to deportation had been apprehended. Sixty-four of them agreed to depart voluntarily and were taken to the Mexican border by truck, while the rest were held for formal warrant proceedings. The latter category, of course, held a number of Chinese, Japanese, and Caucasians, but in Watkins' words, it was "the Mexican element which predominates."[28]

The Mexican and other ethnic communities were not about to take the investigations passively. La Opinion railed against the raids, while ethnic brotherhood associations gave advice and assistance. A meeting of over one hundred Mexican and Mexican-American businessmen on the evening of February 16 resulted in the organization of the Mexican Chamber of Commerce in Los Angeles, and a pledge to carry complaints about the treatment of

---

[26] Los Angeles Examiner, Los Angeles Times, and Los Angeles La Opinion, Feb. 15, 1931; see also Los Angeles Evening Express, Feb. 16, 1931.

[27] Watkins to White, Feb. 21, 1931, NA RG 85, file 55739/674.

[28] Ibid. Aliens who left under voluntary departure could theoretically apply for admission to the United States legally; deported aliens at that time were barred from reentry.

Mexican nationals to both Mexico City and Washington, D.C. Mexican merchants in Los Angeles, who catered to the trade of their ethnic group, felt that their business had been adversely affected, since Mexicans living in outlying areas now hesitated to present themselves in Los Angeles for possible harassment. Sheriff Traeger's deputies in particular were criticized for rounding up Mexicans in large groups and taking them to jail without checking whether anyone in the group had a passport. Consul de la Colina appeared at this meeting as an invited guest, and he promised to uphold the rights of his compatriots before the pressures of immigration officials who acted in so arbitrary a manner.[29]

Consul de la Colina had been working tirelessly on behalf of destitute Mexicans in need of aid or who desired repatriation. Much of his time was occupied with meeting immigration officials who kept assuring him that the Mexicans were not being singled out for deportation. He also warned against unscrupulous individuals who were taking advantage of Mexican nationals by soliciting funds for charity and issuing bogus affidavits to Mexicans who had lost their papers.[30]

Despite the adverse reaction to and public knowledge of the drive on aliens, Watkins persisted. "I am fully convinced that there is an extensive field here for deportation work and as we can gradually absorb same it is expected [*sic*] to ask for additional help," he stated. Responding to the charges of dragnet methods, he notified his superiors in Washington:

I have tried to be extremely careful to avoid the holding of aliens by or for this Service who are not deportable and to this end it is our endeavor to immediately release at the local point of investigation any alien who is not found to be deportable as soon as his examination is completed.[31]

The tension cooled briefly as the immigration officials held off making further raids for a few days, and Carr and Watkins issued a new statement giving assurance that they intended no persecution of a particular ethnic group. Only aliens illegally in the country

---

29 *Los Angeles Evening Express,* Feb. 17, 1931; Los Angeles *La Opinion,* Feb. 16, 1931; *Los Angeles Record,* Feb. 24, 1931.
30 Los Angeles *La Opinion,* Feb. 17, 19, and 28, 1931.
31 Watkins to White, Feb. 21, 1931, NA RG 85, file 55739/674.

were to be deported.[32] This statement may be contrasted with the one released to the papers by Carr on January 30. The Spanish-speaking community must have found the contradictions baffling, as official pronouncements of fair treatment alternated with intensive prosecutions.[33]

The controversy was renewed on February 26 when Watkins' agents, assisted by over two dozen Los Angeles policemen, surrounded the downtown Plaza at three o'clock in the afternoon. About 400 people were detained within the grounds of the small circular park for over an hour. Eleven Mexicans, five Chinese, and a Japanese were held; nine of the Mexicans were released the following day. Although the Los Angeles metropolitan newspapers ignored the raid, a *La Opinion* photographer took a picture of the proceedings, and the Spanish-language paper gave the raid extensive, if hostile, coverage.[34] Watkins decided that the idea of "conducting investigations at fixed places, which the newspapers term 'raids,' are not proving particularly successful," especially because "in this city large numbers of contraband aliens are not frequently found in one place." After this Watkins planned to have his men work in small groups, as secretly as possible, concentrating on the county's outlying districts.[35]

The procedures that Watkins followed in detaining aliens, holding them without benefit of counsel, and telegraphing for a warrant of arrest *after* a provable case was found, were standard methods in 1931. Not until 1933 would changes be made and basic civil liberties extended to aliens.[36] It has been noted that Watkins reported to his superiors in Washington that he made every effort to release innocent people as soon as possible, which in practice might not have been for several days. The deportation drive on a national level received heavy criticism on this point from liberal magazines, civil libertarians, and the Wickersham Commission on law observance and enforcement.[37]

---

32 *Los Angeles Evening Express*, Feb. 19, 1931.

33 The uncertainty is reflected by the Los Angeles *La Opinion*, which announced a raid on February 15, a promise of amity four days later, another raid on February 22, another promise three days later, and still another raid on February 27.

34 Los Angeles *La Opinion*, Feb. 27 and 28, 1931.

35 Watkins to White, March 2, 1931, NA RG 85, file 55739/674.

36 U.S. Secretary of Labor, *Twenty-Second Annual Report of the Secretary of Labor* (Washington, 1934), 1551–1552.

37 National Commission on Law Observance and Enforcement, "Report on En-

By March 7 Watkins had received 138 warrants for deportation proceedings. Of this number, 80 were intended for Mexican aliens, 19 for Japanese, 8 for Chinese, and the remainder for "miscellaneous nationalities." In addition to these aliens, Watkins allowed 80 other aliens who were found to be deportable to leave for the Mexican border under the "voluntary departure" option, transportation courtesy of the federal government. Noting that arrests in early March had noticeably declined "due to concealment and elopement of aliens," Watkins dispatched eleven agents to visit other parts of the district, and went himself to Bakersfield for further investigatory work.[38] The federal deportation drive thus departed from southern California, though the local immigration office continued to arrest deportable aliens as part of its routine tasks.

The final figures listed by Watkins on April 22, 1931, were 230 aliens deported by formal proceedings, of whom 110 were Mexican nationals, with 159 additional voluntary departures to Mexico. Since these figures reveal that seven out of ten persons deported in the southern California anti-alien drive were Mexicans, the conclusion seems inescapable that the Mexican community there had every reason to express its concern. By the supervisor's own admission, in order to capture the 389 aliens successfully prosecuted, Watkins and his men had to round up and question somewhere between 3,000 and 4,000 people.[39]

Mexican consular officers had statistics of their own, which might be contrasted with the work of the immigration service. Consul de la Colina intervened on behalf of his government in 1,216 cases involving possible deportation in 1931. The following year the number for Los Angeles was down to 212. Consular offices in other cities with large Spanish-speaking elements reported far fewer interventions than had occurred in Los Angeles during 1931. El Paso's consul had 171 cases; there were 152 in Houston, 52 in Chicago, 28 in Detroit, and 124 in Phoenix.[40]

forcement of Deportation Laws of U.S.," 154; editorial in *Nation*, CXXXIII (Aug. 19, 1931), 170; editorial in *New Republic*, LXVIII (Aug. 19, 1931), 2; Reuben Oppenheimer, "The Deportation Terror," *New Republic*, LXIX (Jan. 13, 1932), 231–234.

[38] Telegram from Watkins to White, March 7, 1931, NA RG 85, file 55739/674.

[39] Watkins to Visel, April 22, 1931, Clements Papers, and Watkins to White, Feb. 21, 1931, NA RG 85, file 55739/674.

[40] Secretaría de Relaciones Exteriores, *Apendice a la Memoria de la Secretaría de Relaciones Exteriores de Agosto de 1931 a Julio de 1932* (Mexico, 1932), table facing p. 984.

Doak's anti-alien drive not only failed to solve the unemployment problem; it created new tensions and accelerated hostile attitudes. The Department of Labor continued its pressure on deportable aliens, though the circumspection of career officials probably aided the campaign more than the verbal blasts periodically issued by Doak.[41] Even Visel, in congratulating the Department of Labor for endorsing his idea, found that the Labor Department had decided it had generated enough publicity in Los Angeles. Assistant Secretary W. W. Husband, who acknowledged Visel's letter, stated, "It is the purpose of this Department that the deportation provisions of our immigration laws shall be carried out to the fullest possible extent but the Department is equally desirous that such activities shall be carried out strictly in accordance with law." Cooperation by local authorities was appreciated; but Husband made it clear that from the viewpoint of the federal government it was the local authority that was supposed to respond to the federal government's initiative in the enforcement of federal laws, not the other way around.[42] The sequence of events in Los Angeles, however, had made such a point an academic one.

The effect of the drive on the Mexican community in Los Angeles was traumatic. Many of the aliens apprehended had never regularized an illegal entry that might have been made years before, at a time when no penalties for illegal entry were even provided for by law. Other than that, to call them criminals is to misapply the term. The pressure on the Mexican community contributed significantly to the huge repatriation movement from Los Angeles that followed upon the anti-alien drive. Beginning in March 1931, the Los Angeles County Bureau of Welfare inaugurated a series of repatriation trains to transport indigent Mexican families as far as Mexico City. By the end of the year four shipments had taken over 2,300 people, including American-born children, out of the country. A similar, though uncounted, number left during 1931 with the aid of the Mexican consulate and charitable Spanish-speaking organizations. Many others went to other regions in the United States. Estimates

---

41 *New York Times*, July 17, 1931; U.S. Commissioner General of Immigration, *Annual Report of the Commissioner General of Immigration, 1931* (Washington, 1931), 13; see also report for 1932, pp. 2–3.

42 Husband to Visel, March 27, 1931, NA RG 85, file 55739/674.

of the exodus from southern California varied between 50,000 and 75,000 people during 1931.[43] Such a mass movement of people, until now barely mentioned in historical studies, indicates the degree of work yet to be done by scholars in the writing of Mexican-American history.

---

[43] *Los Angeles Evening Express,* Aug. 18, 1931; *New York Times,* Feb. 7, 1932; *Los Angeles Record,* March 7, 1932; Los Angeles County Department of Charities, "Analysis of Mexican Repatriation Trains," June 15, 1934, copy in NA RG 59, file 311.1215 /65. Reports of mass deportations, and the plight of deportees and repatriates stranded in such border towns as Mexicali and Ciudad Juárez, prompted the Mexican embassy to inquire what the Bureau of Immigration was doing in Los Angeles. See Secretary of State Henry L. Stimpson to Doak, May 27, 1931, enclosing a note from the Mexican embassy, dated May 7, 1931, NA RG 85, file 55739/674; and Hoffman, "Repatriation of Mexican Nationals," 113–120.

From Discrimination to Repatriation: Mexican Life in Gary, Indiana, During the Great Depression

Neil Betten and
Raymond A. Mohl

Mr. Betten is a member of the history department in Florida State University and Mr. Mohl is a member of the history department in Florida Atlantic University.

During the past decade Americans have been rediscovering important parts of their past. With a few notable exceptions, Mexican Americans—the nation's second largest minority—until recently rated very little space in scholarly writing in history and the social sciences. Today, however, historians and others have begun to probe the experience of Mexicans north of the border.[1] The history of Mexican immigrants in the United States has not been a particularly happy one. Sought primarily as cheap laborers and subjected to poverty and discrimination, Mexicans nevertheless migrated to the United States in large numbers, especially after World War I, as restrictive quotas in the 1920s cut off the flow of Euro-

[1] Paul S. Taylor, Emory S. Bogardus, Carey McWilliams, and Manuel Gamio were among early scholars who examined the Mexican experience in the United States. See Paul S. Taylor's multi-volume study, *Mexican Labor in the United States* (Berkeley, Calif., 1928–1934; reprinted, New York, 1966–1968); Emory S. Bogardus, *The Mexican Immigrant* (Los Angeles, 1929); Emory S. Bogardus, *The Mexican in the United States* (Los Angeles, 1934); Carey McWilliams, *North from Mexico: The Spanish-Speaking People of the United States* (Philadelphia, 1949); Manuel Gamio, *Mexican Immigration to the United States: A Study of Human Migration and Adjustment* (Chicago,

pean immigrants. But with the Great Depression of the 1930s, Mexicans bore the brunt of nativist hostilities and suffered massive deportations. These patterns prevailed not only in the Southwest, where most Mexican immigrants resided, but also in northern industrial cities like Gary, Indiana, where substantial Mexican colonies had sprouted during the 1920s.

Mexicans migrated to northwest Indiana to labor in the steel mills of Gary and nearby East Chicago. With the outbreak of World War I and the virtual suspension of European immigration, U. S. Steel and other corporations began drawing Mexican workers from Texas, Kansas, and Mexico to fill factory jobs. The pace of Mexican migration to the area speeded up during the steel strike of 1919 when the corporations recruited Mexican strike breakers from as far away as Laredo and El Paso. By 1920 fifteen major industrial plants in the Gary–Chicago region employed 1,746 Mexicans; another 868 Mexicans worked on local railroads. Although some out-migration occurred during the recession of 1921, Mexican migration to the area passed all previous totals during the mid-1920s. By 1926 East Chicago's Inland Steel employed 2,526 Mexican workers, representing thirty-five percent of its labor unit. According to the 1930 census, some 9,007 Mexican-born immigrants lived in Lake County, Indiana—almost all of them in Gary and East Chicago.[2]

1930); Manuel Gamio, *The Mexican Immigrant: His Life Story* (Chicago, 1931). Indicative of awakened interest in Mexican-American history is the recent and important volume, Leo Grebler, *et al.*, *The Mexican-American People: The Nation's Second Largest Minority* (New York, 1970). See also the issues of the *Journal of Mexican American History*, *El Grito*, and *Aztlán*. For a recent study of repatriation in the Los Angeles area, see Abraham Hoffman, "Stimulus to Repatriation: The 1931 Federal Deportation Drive and the Los Angeles Mexican Community," *Pacific Historical Review*, XLII (1973), 205–219.

2 Powell A. Moore, *The Calumet Region: Indiana's Last Frontier* (Indianapolis, 1959), 252, 342, 395–396; Julian Samora and Richard A. Lamanna, *Mexican-Americans in a Midwest Metropolis: A Study of East Chicago* (University of California, Los Angeles, Mexican-American Study Project, Advance Report No. 8, 1967), 71; Paul S. Taylor, "Mexican Labor in the United States: Chicago and the Calumet Region," *University of California Publications in Economics*, VII (1932), 61; Paul S. Taylor, "Employment of Mexicans in Chicago and the Calumet Region," *Journal of the American Statistical Association*, XXV (June, 1930), 206–207; U.S. Bureau of the Census, *Fifteenth Census of the United States, 1930: Population* (Washington, D. C., 1932), III, Part 1, p. 720. For more general studies of Mexican immigration, see José Hernández Alvarez, "A Demographic Profile of the Mexican Immigration to the United States, 1910–1950," *Journal of Inter-American Studies*, VIII (1966), 471–496; Paul S. Taylor, "Some Aspects of Mexican Immigration," *Journal of Political Economy*, XXXVIII (1930), 609–615; Paul S. Taylor, "Note on Streams of Mexican Migration," *American*

The Mexicans who migrated to Gary and the Calumet Region of Indiana faced rather persistent patterns of discrimination and often found it difficult to overcome the social results of poverty. The problem of housing provides a case in point. Planned and built between 1906 and 1909 by a U. S. Steel subsidiary, the Gary Land Company, Gary quickly developed a sprawling slum of shacks, barrack-like boarding houses, and cheap frame houses filled with immigrant workers and their families. Early planners had divided the city and assigned workers to neighborhoods according to their jobs. The Gary Land Company reserved one section of the city for management and supervisory personnel, other sections for the primarily American-born foremen, skilled workers, and clerical staff; the company left little space for the unskilled immigrants who formed the bulk of the work force.[3] Some of the early Mexican recruits were originally housed in company boarding houses adjacent to the mills, but the arrangement was not entirely satisfactory. Mexican workers found themselves subjected to employer supervision during non-working hours. They soon discovered that the corporations charged more for housing and food than private boarding house keepers. Moreover, Mexicans living in company boarding houses often complained of harassment by Gary police in nearby downtown streets. Ironically, they had greater freedom in Gary's less controlled but hardly idyllic industrial slum. Preferring to board with their own people and eat familiar food, Mexican workers quickly moved from corporation facilities. By 1928 none of the Gary plants housed Mexican workers.[4]

Mexican immigrant workers who left company barracks, like

Journal of Sociology, XXXVI (1930), 287–288; "Increase of Mexican Population in the United States, 1920–1930," *Monthly Labor Review*, XXXVII (July 1933), 45–48; "Mexican Immigration," *Transactions of the Commonwealth Club of California*, XXI (March 1926), 1–34. For specific studies of Mexicans in northern cities, see " 'Little Mexico' in North Cities," *World's Work*, XLVIII (1924), 466; Ruth Camblon, "Mexicans in Chicago," *The Family*, VII (1926), 207–211; Anita E. Jones, "Mexican Colonies in Chicago," *Social Service Review*, II (1928), 579–597; Norman D. Humphrey, "The Migration and Settlement of Detroit Mexicans," *Economic Geography*, XIX (1943), 358–361; T. Earl Sullenger, "The Mexican Population of Omaha," *Journal of Applied Sociology*, VIII (1924), 289–293.

3 On the early planning of Gary, see Raymond A. Mohl and Neil Betten, "The Failure of Industrial City Planning: Gary, Indiana, 1906–1910," *Journal of the American Institute of Planners*, XXXVIII (1972), 203–215.

4 Moore, *The Calumet Region*, 396–397; *Gary Post-Tribune*, May 24, 1923; interview with steelworker Victor Valdez, Gary, Indiana, August 1970.

blacks and east and south European immigrants unable to find other housing, crowded into Gary's "south side"—an unplanned section south of U. S. Steel property but within the corporate limits of the city. The area had no municipal services for many years, and no city housing or zoning ordinances restricted cheap and shabby construction by real estate speculators and builders. Inadequate and overcrowded housing, high crime rates, and health problems (especially pneumonia and tuberculosis) plagued the area, even in the relatively good times of the 1920s. The Mexican consul in Chicago visited Gary in 1924 and depicted Mexican living and housing conditions as indescribably wretched. The following year an investigatory committee of a local women's club was shocked by the "congestion of humanity" in Mexican neighborhoods. The committee's report especially deplored the higher rents paid by Mexicans (and blacks) for housing considerably more shabby than that of white residents in the same area. It also noted that the State Board of Health had condemned some occupied structures. Even in sound buildings many Mexican families lived in filthy, damp basements without adequate facilities. At the end of the 1920s a social worker from Gary's Neighborhood House, a Presbyterian settlement, described a typical Mexican family as living in a tiny basement apartment, lacking any furniture save a box which served as a table; "they slept on the floor as they had in Mexico."[5]

These conditions worsened during the depression of the following decade. For the Mexican community, the economic breakdown meant increased poverty as Gary's industry came to a virtual standstill. All local workers faced similar problems, but Gary's Mexicans —like its blacks—came to the area last, had few saleable skills, and faced employment discrimination. With income low and unemployment high, problems mounted. According to the *Gary Post-Tribune*, tuberculosis and rickets reached epidemic proportions in the Mexican community. Social agencies found malnutrition endemic among Mexican children. Although admitting that undernourishment and cramped living were important causes for Mexican health problems, one local newspaper believed that the cold

---

[5] *Gary Post-Tribune*, April 24, 1924, Feb. 24, 1925; Marie Prather, "Housing Survey," *Americans All* (May 1925), 5–6; Gary Neighborhood House, *Twenty Years of Neighborliness* (Gary, n.d., ca. 1930), unpaginated pamphlet.

climate was the major reason for Mexican susceptibility to disease. In December 1930 Gary's International Institute, an immigrant-oriented welfare agency sponsored by the Y.W.C.A., reported that Mexicans far outnumbered any other nationality in terms of unemployment, housing, and health problems. In a second report, the Institute lamented that Mexicans "are the least rooted in the community, and consequently are less equipped to meet this period of depression through which we are passing. . . . The agony and suffering that all of these people endure is beyond comprehension of any who have not experienced it."[6]

Poverty magnified the daily discrimination faced by Mexicans. During the depression, local white antagonism culminated in a government campaign of threats and harassment against Mexican workers. Indeed, the open hostility towards them in the thirties drew upon the blatant racism of earlier decades. In 1921 an International Institute worker depicted anti-Mexican feelings stemming from skin color: "The Mexican girl is rather lonely in Gary. The white girl looks upon her as colored while she in turn regards the colored girl the same as the white girl does." In 1924 another social worker, Marie Prather, aptly described anti-Mexican bigotry in Gary: "Americans seem to consider all Mexicans like the famous Villa who was so much talked of a few years ago. . . . Newspapers are partly to blame. . . . Then, too, because of the very dark color of most Mexicans, Americans have the same racial feelings as they have for the colored."[7]

Obvious discrimination occurred in housing. Although Mexicans might rent apartments or buy substandard homes at exorbitant rates

[6] *Gary Post-Tribune,* Feb. 24, 1932, p. 9; International Institute, Monthly Reports, Oct. 1929, Dec. 1930, May 1931, Gary International Institute Papers, International Institute, 725 East 5th Avenue, Gary (hereafter referred to as I.I. Papers). See also Benjamin Goldberg, "Tuberculosis in Racial Types with Special Reference to Mexicans," *American Journal of Public Health,* XIX (1929), 274–286, which reaffirmed the general image of Mexican immigrants as tubercular and diseased. The Gary International Institute, like similarly named agencies in over sixty cities, aided immigrants in adjusting to American society and in preserving their cultural heritage. Originating as branches of local Young Women's Christian Associations, especially in post-World War I years, the institutes became virtually autonomous, drawing their staffs largely from local immigrants. See Raymond A. Mohl and Neil Betten, "Ethnic Adjustment in the Industrial City: The International Institute of Gary, 1919–1940," *International Migration Review,* VI (1972), 361–376.

[7] Monthly Report, Oct. 1921, I. I. Papers; Marie Prather to Mrs. Bruno Lasker, May 12, 1924, Correspondence file, 1919–1929, *ibid.*

on the south side, it was practically impossible to rent in "better" parts of Gary. "On the north side they will not rent to Mexicans," said a Mexican immigrant in the late 1920s. "We don't care about it; we couldn't pay the rent they charge down there anyway." But many did care, whether the discrimination affected them personally or not. Another Gary Mexican told how he could rent only after passing as a non-Mexican. In another case a fair-complexioned, light-haired Mexican steel worker with an Anglicized name arranged to buy a home in the middle-class Tolleston district. When the real estate agent saw his darker wife and children and realized they were Mexicans, he refused to complete the transaction. However, if the worker had provided the agent with a sizeable bribe and agreed "to deny my Mexican nationality," a deal could have been made. The agent felt that, if he could claim the family was Spanish rather than Mexican, he would not violate the unwritten local codes of his profession. Such housing discrimination continued at least into the late 1940s.[8]

Other forms of discrimination existed as well. The police harassment prevalent during the twenties continued into the thirties. The Hotel Gary, the city's only major hotel during the depression, refused to admit Mexicans. Mexicans often found sales clerks hostile in Gary retail stores. Formal segregation of Mexicans in Gary theaters had ended in 1925 (it continued in East Chicago through the 1930s), but some Mexicans still felt, as one retired worker recently put it, "unwelcome and unwanted in the Gary movie houses." Many Gary Mexicans, especially young male workers, preferred to travel to Chicago for entertainment.[9]

Even participation in church life proved a hurdle for the Mexican community. Although most of Gary's Catholic ethnic groups established their own parishes, Mexicans did not do so until 1924. While many Mexicans preferred their own parish, others resented having to attend a special church. Within the Mexican church, some friction existed between the Mexican parishioners and Catholic priests. The story of one man's experience suggests the extent of this clerical problem. After coming to Gary, this Mexican steel

---

8 Taylor, "Mexican Labor in the United States," 226–227; interview with James Wright, a Mexican steelworker, Gary, Indiana, Aug. 1970.

9 Interview with Jesús López, Gary, Indiana, Jan. 1971; Chicago *Mexico*, March 21, 1925, p. 1; Taylor, "Mexican Labor in the United States," 232.

worker first attended the Catholic church closest to his residence, but was directed to another, being told it was "better for Mexicans." Upon attending the acceptable church he found that, unlike in Mexico where he could attend or not and still be considered part of the parish, here he would have to be an active church member. In Mexico, he said, "we just went to church and it didn't cost anything if we didn't have money. Here it cost twenty-five cents at the door and twenty-five cents in the plate." In Gary he felt obligated to contribute and, therefore, did not attend church regularly because "it was too much money at that time." Not being in regular attendance meant "I could not be buried by the church, nor receive last rites." He claimed that two close friends who were not church members, and perhaps anti-clerical, were denied last rites by the local priest. Another Mexican steel worker, who now holds a leadership position in his United Steelworkers local, revealed that for a time the local priest refused to baptize children of Mexican parents who did not attend church. Many of these problems stemmed from the fact that the priests in the Mexican church were non-Mexican. Perhaps the priest's loyalty to his own ethnic group, or his unconscious prejudice against a people with darker skins, or the frustration of ministering to a reluctant flock led to conflict. Unlike east European immigrants in Gary, Mexicans had an anti-clerical tradition which intensified under the pressures of migration and industrial life.[10]

Mexican laborers, as noted earlier, also faced discrimination from employers. The resentment of the workers was intense, but most of them aimed their complaints at immediate non-Mexican superiors rather than at the corporations themselves. This pattern of antagonism emerged largely because of the industry's practice of providing low-level supervisors with considerable disciplinary power in order to foster high production levels. Mexican workers complained that the foreman's own ethnic group received the best work assignments, and when someone had to be laid off, it would be a Mexican or a black, but never one of the foreman's people. As one steel worker put it, "The *mayordomos* make distinctions. They give the Mex-

---

[10] Interview with James Wright, Gary, Indiana, Aug. 1970; interview with Joseph Alimillo, Gary, Indiana, Aug. 1970. See also Gamio, *Mexican Immigration to the United States,* 112–122; and Edwin R. Brown, "The Challenge of Mexican Immigration," *Missionary Review of the World,* XLIX (1926), 192–196.

icans the heavy work and the Poles *suave* work with better pay." He added, "The office [management] makes no distinctions." Another worker agreed that "the company is all right," but added that it "never know[s] what the foremen do. A lot of the foremen take five dollars or ten dollars from men to get them good jobs at the mill. That is the way the new men get good jobs and we get moved to other jobs." Many Mexicans also resorted to bribery to retain jobs. Economist Paul Taylor's well-known 1932 study of Mexicans in the Gary–Chicago area found that employment managers of steel mills readily admitted discriminatory hiring and firing. "When I hire Mexicans at the gate," said one employment manager, "I pick out the lightest among them. No, it isn't that the lighter-colored ones are any better workers, but the darker ones are like the niggers." Another noted that "when employment slackens the Mexicans are the first ones off. They are not Americans."[11]

Nation-wide discrimination against Mexicans, as well as local hostility, both before and during the depression, prepared the Gary population for the forced exodus—called "repatriation"—of a large portion of the Mexican community during the early 1930s. Mexicans, along with other aliens and unnaturalized immigrants, emerged as scapegoats of the depression. American nativists urged deportation of immigrants and "undesirable aliens" to renew capitalist prosperity. The widely read *Saturday Evening Post* promoted this brand of depression nativism in a number of anti-immigrant articles.[12] Similarly, Congressman Martin Dies, writing in the *Chicago Herald-Examiner*, spoke for numerous nativists in declaring that the "large alien population is the basic cause of unemployment." Throughout the United States the new nativists joined "patriotic" organizations designed to keep America pure: the Allied Patriotic Society, the Rhode Island Association of Patriots, the Westchester Security League, the Chicago Women's Ideal Club, the Patriotic American Civic Alliance, the Old Glory Club of Flatbush. According to pro-immigrant writer Louis Adamic, most such groups

---

11 Taylor, "Mexican Labor in the United States," 90, 92, 101–102, 110; interview with Joseph Alimillo, Gary, Indiana, Aug. 1970.

12 See, for example, Raymond G. Carroll, "The Alien on Relief," *Saturday Evening Post*, CCVIII (Jan. 11, 1936), 16–17, 100–103; Raymond G. Carroll, "Alien Workers in America," *ibid.* (Jan. 25, 1936), 32, 82–89; Raymond G. Carroll, "Aliens in Subversive Activities," *ibid.* (Feb. 22, 1936), 10–11, 84–90; Isaac F. Marcosson, "The Alien in America," *ibid.*, CCVII (April 6, 1935), 22–23.

believed that the best way to end the depression lay in the deportation of all aliens.[13]

Nativists throughout the country directed much of their hostile energies against the Mexican immigrant. Most immigrants from Mexico retained their Mexican citizenship and thus seemed clearly to fit the alien image. Undoubtedly, the Mexican's darker skin color, his Catholicism, and the usual problems and vices associated with the poor and exploited affected national opinion as well. Raymond G. Carroll, a journalist and the *Saturday Evening Post's* major propagandist on the subject, considered Mexicans "the most unassimilable of aliens." He accused Mexicans of filling up depression relief rolls and investing public assistance funds in moneymaking schemes. Carroll rather curiously concluded that the poverty-ridden Mexican immigrant "is bountifully fed and housed, whether he works or not." Economist Roy L. Garis, writing on "The Mexican Invasion" in the *Post,* depicted Mexicans as lazy and inferior immigrants who dangerously threatened American stock. In a 1929 editorial, the *Post* attacked Mexican immigration and labelled the new migrants "a most undesirable ethnic stock for the melting pot."[14]

The generally hostile attitude of native Americans, buttressed by the anti-Mexican rhetoric of the *Saturday Evening Post,* stimulated the repatriation movement in every major Mexican community in the United States. As the depression deepened, the repatriation movement intensified. In an exacting study, historian Abraham Hoffman recently concluded that well over 400,000 Mexicans (or about one-third of the Mexicans in the United States in 1930) were repatriated between 1929 and 1935. A disproportionate number left from the midwestern states bordering on Lake Michigan.

13 *Chicago Herald-Examiner,* undated clipping, Alien Restriction folder, I.I. Papers; Louis Adamic, "Aliens and Alien-Baiters," *Harpers Magazine,* CLXXIII (Nov. 1936), 567–569, 571. On the anti-immigrant activities of Martin Dies, see *New York Times,* Feb. 1, 1935, p. 28, June 23, 1935, p. 1, Feb. 16, 1936, part IV, p. 11, March 21, 1937, p. 9; William Gellerman, *Martin Dies* (New York, 1944), 49–53.

14 Carroll, "Alien Workers in America," 87–88; Carroll, "The Alien on Relief," 12; Roy L. Garis, "The Mexican Invasion," *Saturday Evening Post,* CCII (April 19, 1930), 44; "Mexican Conquest," *ibid.,* CCI (June 22, 1929), 26. These writers drew upon the pronounced anti-Mexican attitudes of the intolerant twenties. See, for example, Kenneth L. Roberts, "Wet and Other Mexicans," *Saturday Evening Post,* CC (Feb. 4, 1928), 10–11, 137–146; Kenneth L. Roberts, "Mexicans or Ruin," *ibid.* (Feb. 18, 1928), 14–15, 142–154; Kenneth L. Roberts, "The Docile Mexican," *ibid.* (March 10, 1928), 39–41.

Paul S. Taylor found that while 3.6 percent of Mexican nationals in the United States lived in Indiana, Michigan, and Illinois, this region provided over 10 percent of the repatriates.[15]

Arguments favoring repatriation seldom differed. Few failed to note that unemployed Mexicans boosted relief costs during the depression. Others contended that nearly bankrupt towns and cities could not afford school programs for Mexican children. For a small initial outlay, a Mexican family could be shipped back to Mexico, thus saving money for taxpayers. Americans also argued that Mexicans wanted to return, that the Mexican government wanted them back and would provide jobs or land, and that Mexicans preferred poverty at home to degradation in a strange land like the United States.[16]

An examination of Mexican repatriation in Gary illuminates the consistencies, as well as the fallacies, in contemporary rationalizations for the mass removal. Local newspapers in the Calumet Region fully backed repatriation, suggested that the Mexican communities completely endorsed the idea, and depicted the trips as having a holiday atmosphere. The local elite in the community added significant support for repatriation. Just as Inland Steel encouraged repatriation of Mexicans in East Chicago, so did U. S. Steel in Gary. In fact, Horace S. Norton, superintendent of U. S. Steel's Gary Works and president of the Gary Chamber of Commerce, emerged as the major spokesman for repatriation. "The kindest thing which could be done [for] these people would be to send them back to Mexico," Norton said in 1932. "They do not assimilate and are unhappy here. They want to go back and I understand that Mexico welcomes them." He disavowed any U. S. Steel

---

15 Abraham Hoffman, "The Repatriation of Mexican Nationals from the United States during the Great Depression" (Ph.D. dissertation, University of California, Los Angeles, 1970), vii, 185, 225; Paul S. Taylor, "Mexican Labor in the United States: Migration Statistics," *University of California Publications in Economics*, XII (1934), 48. See also Emory S. Bogardus, "Mexican Repatriates," *Sociology and Social Research*, XVIII (1933), 169–176; John H. Burma, *Spanish-Speaking Groups in the United States* (Durham, N.C., 1954), 13–44; Grebler, *et al.*, *The Mexican-American People*, 523–526; *New York Times*, Oct. 30, 1931, p. 6, Dec. 8, 1931, p. 22, July 9, 1932, p. 7; Norman D. Humphrey, "Mexican Repatriation from Michigan: Public Assistance in Historical Perspective," *Social Service Review*, XV (1941), 497–513.

16 For typical arguments favoring repatriation, see *Gary Post-Tribune*, Jan. 14, 1932, p. 1, Feb. 27, 1932, p. 1, March 16, 1932, p. 1, May 11, 1932, p. 1, Nov. 1, 1932, p. 1, Nov. 9, 1932, p. 9.

responsibility for Mexican migration to Gary: "I personally know that no Lake County industrial concern made any effort to get them to come here. . . . The majority just drifted in." Other civic leaders, such as H. B. Snyder, president of the Gary Reconstruction Association, Walter J. Riley, head of the Twin City Manufacturers Organization, and John Malme, chairman of the Committee of Ten and the Gary Relief Committee, also endorsed the plan. Another steel executive, Eugene G. Grace, president of Bethlehem Steel, backhandedly praised Mexican labor as willing "to work hard, and return to their homeland when need for them has past." The steel city of Gary sought to fulfill this prophecy.[17]

Repatriation from Gary passed through two distinct phases—one voluntary, the other much less so. From 1931 to May 1932 repatriation was voluntary. When the Mexican government invited its nationals to return, implying that they would improve economically by doing so, many immigrants readily took this avenue of escape from the destitution brought on by the temporary collapse of the American economy. As Robert N. McLean, a Presbyterian missionary among Mexicans in California, put it in an article discussing repatriation on the national scale, "Vicente is sure that a kind government is waiting to make him a landowner, and to stake him to a start." McLean quoted a voluntary repatriate: "If you were broke and without a job, would you be rather home, or in a foreign country?" Another repatriate noted that "in Mexico there was always beans and tortillas. . . . In the United States if you have no money, you starve." The situation in Gary, at least until mid-1932, bore out McLean's impression about the voluntary nature of repatriation.[18]

During the early years of the depression, many Mexicans in Gary voluntarily returned to their homeland. By the summer of 1931 Gary's International Institute reported that "many Mexicans have left Gary via trucks, old automobiles, and on foot returning to Mexico." The Institute added that "a goodly proportion of those remaining in Gary would return to Mexico if it were financially possible." "Many who have no savings and have no work or prospects of any are very anxious to leave before another winter sets in." In

---

[17] *Gary Post-Tribune,* Jan. 14, 1932, p. 4, May 12, 1932, p. 1; Hammond *Lake County Times,* May 12, 1932, p. 1.

[18] Robert N. McLean, "Goodbye, Vicente!" *Survey,* LXVI (May 1, 1931), 195, 196.

September, the Institute noted that "many are returning in trucks, such a large number going on one truck they have to stand, and only a few days ago one of the Mexicans who left Gary in this way was thrown from the truck and killed before the border was reached." Responding to these hardships, the Institute sought free transportation for returning Mexicans from Gary's Council of Social Agencies, but without success. However, the Institute did secure free passes on Mexican railroads for voluntary repatriates through the aid of Rafael Aveleyra, the Mexican consul in Chicago.[19] Many Mexicans also asked the United States government for help in returning home. The files of the International Institute contain numerous requests from those seeking government aid. The Institute's executive secretary complained in June 1931 that "many Mexicans in Gary are applying for [subsidized] voluntary removal but to date the Immigration Office has received none of the appropriation to send them."[20]

The International Institute's involvement in repatriation alarmed the agency's national office—the YWCA Department of Immigration and Foreign Communities. "Our experience from other places has been that the immigration authorities are only too eager to sent [sic] all eligible applicants and order their removal," Aghavnie Yegenian of the YWCA's national board wrote. She added that "in some places it has been reported to us that Mexicans have been forced against their will to go when they have applied for relief to city departments of public welfare." Isabel Rogers of the Gary Institute confidently answered, "we know of no instance here that the Mexicans ... have been forced against their will to go when they have applied for public relief." Rogers soon changed her mind as repatriation in Gary became involuntary.[21]

In 1932 a community-wide program promoting forced repatriation began in Gary. It was designed by a coalition of groups with mixed and sometimes conflicting motives: businessmen seeking to

---

19 Isabel Rogers to A. Y. Yegenian, Aug. 17, 1931, I.I. Papers; Monthly Reports, May, September, 1931, *ibid.*; Annual Report, 1931, *ibid.*

20 Isabel Rogers to Florence G. Cassidy, June 18, 1931, Correspondence file, 1930–1934, *ibid.*; Ethel Bird to A. Y. Yegenian, May 7, 1931, *ibid.* See also Monthly Reports, 1931–1932, *ibid.*

21 A. Y. Yegenian to Isabel Rogers, Aug. 12, 1931, *ibid.*; Rogers to Yegenian, Aug. 17, 1931, *ibid.*

lower taxes, nativists aiming to rid the area of Mexicans, township trustee officials intending to cut relief costs, and International Institute social workers hoping to find their Mexican clientele better economic conditions in Mexico. Private fund-raising financed the first trips back to Mexico. The press stressed savings to the community and the generosity of the railroads. One newspaper gave the cost for transportation of one family to Mexico as $37.50—a "charity rate" provided by the railroads. Each family on relief cost the township $336 a year. Thus, the paper argued, for an "investment" of $37.50 the more costly relief charges could be eliminated. This rationale had first been presented by a local branch of the American Legion, original sponsors of publicly financed Mexican repatriation in northwest Indiana. Township trustee Mary Grace Wells contended that it "would be a blessing to the community, a kindness to them to help them go back home." Maria Candeleria of the International Institute appealed for economic support because "almost every case is tubercular or otherwise diseased and . . . constitute[s] a serious health problem."[22]

Repatriation advocates raised transportation money through a stag party featuring gambling and other attractions. The Knights of Columbus provided facilities for the occasion. "Housewives and others who might object to all the men in town devoting a part of this night to community uplift," the Gary Post-Tribune suggested, "will be urged to make the sacrifice as a civic and patriotic duty." The newspaper frequently pointed out that "proceeds will go to a worthy cause—that of unofficially deporting Mexicans from Gary to reduce the amount of poor relief." The funds collected from the party, supplemented by contributions from individuals and settlement houses, paid for the first trips. Women and children went by train, men by truck. By the end of March, however, private funds seemed exhausted, for the International Institute reported the improbability of additional large groups leaving. Nevertheless, in a short time, the resourceful elite of Gary devised a more efficient system to finance the Mexican exodus.[23]

In May of 1932, Calumet township trustee Mary Grace Wells

---

22 *Gary Post-Tribune,* Jan. 14, 1932, pp. 1, 4, Feb. 4, 1932, p. 1.

23 *Ibid.,* Feb. 5, 1932, p. 1, Feb. 27, 1932, p. 1, March 16, 1932, p. 1; Monthly Report, March 1932, I.I. Papers.

(whose office had responsibility for public assistance) announced a plan to transport all of Gary's remaining unemployed Mexicans back to Mexico. Based on similar practices elsewhere, the Wells plan urged local business to provide her near-bankrupt office with repatriation funds. In turn, the business interests would be reimbursed with scrip which they could use to pay local taxes. Business would lose nothing, and, as Wells pointed out, "it will mean a great saving to the township."[24]

Lake County commissioners responded to the Wells plan by authorizing the removal of every Mexican family receiving public assistance. They further agreed to provide county scrip bearing six percent interest and acceptable for tax payments. Under this plan several trainloads of Mexicans voluntarily left Gary. Either Wells or a representative from her office accompanied each train to the border. After one trip, Wells reported that "all were happy enroute and were delighted to set foot again on their native soil." Other Mexicans continued to emigrate by their own means. The International Institute reported that some returned by car after gasoline money was raised, others in a freight car, and some hitchhiked. One group of Mexican steel workers paid their own way by working "extra days" with the understanding that the income would be used for transportation. During 1932, according to Chairman Walter J. Riley of the Lake County Relief Committee, approximately 1,500 Mexicans were repatriated from Gary, while another 1,800 were sent back from the rest of Lake County; local government financed the trips of more than half and the balance went on their own or with the assistance of private relief agencies.[25]

The first phase of Mexican repatriation in Gary clearly seems voluntary. There is no evidence of Mexican dissatisfaction with repatriation from the city during 1930 and 1931. Many Gary Mexicans who later returned to the United States felt as repatriate Pilar Gómez Norrick did: "repatriation was voluntary [and] . . . there was no other way out. . . . We were happy to leave." The contemporary press sold the program as best it could. A typical headline read,

---

24 *Gary Post-Tribune*, May 11, 1932, p. 1, May 16, 1932, p. 1.

25 *Ibid.*, May 17, 1932, p. 1, July 23, 1932, p. 1, July 26, 1932, p. 1; Monthly Report, May 1932, I.I. Papers; Walter J. Riley, *The Story of Unemployment Relief in Lake County, Indiana* (N.p., 1932), 10.

"150 more Mexicans off on free ride back to Homeland." Likewise, township officials pushed their program. Harry Hutchins, one of the local officials involved, referred to one trip as a "deportation party."[26]

The second phase of Gary's repatriation movement, however, was obviously involuntary. Indeed, after May 1932, when the township trustee's office assumed direction of repatriation, repressive measures were used to force the return of reluctant voyagers. By May the International Institute felt that most of the publicity concerning repatriation tended to discredit Mexicans, "creating the impression that all Mexicans are tubercular, incapable of adjusting themselves to a new country and otherwise undesirable." Much more ominous, noted the Institute, was the fact that "most of those who want to return have already done so, and many of those who remain have been in the U. S. so long they have no close connections in Mexico and no reason for returning." Even the *Gary Post-Tribune* admitted that "some Mexicans have been loath to go back home because they fear they will be unable to find employment." But the newspaper optimistically quoted the Mexican consul in Chicago as saying that there were many employment opportunities. Even so, an investigation carried out by the United States Immigration Office reported that of those families interviewed "none of them desired to return to Mexico."[27]

In September 1932, the Gary International Institute, which had taken no part in the repatriation program since 1931, officially withdrew support. It refused to aid repatriation of aliens unless it could be shown that emigration was purely voluntary and that a specific job awaited each repatriate. A report from the International Institute's national office urged that "no assistance in repatriation be given unless first investigated and ascertained that aliens will be better off in [their] homeland." The Gary Institute agreed: "the report is a confirmation of our own contention that families who have been in this country many years should not be forced to leave." The Gary Institute pointed out that "among the 111 Mexicans who

---

[26] Interview with Pilar Gómez Norrick, Gary, Indiana, Aug. 1970; *Gary Post-Tribune*, Nov. 1, 1932, p. 1, Nov. 9, 1932, p. 9.

[27] Monthly Report, May 1932, I.I. Papers; *Gary Post-Tribune*, April 20, 1932, p. 1, July 23, 1932, p. 1.

left a few days ago were several who went very unwillingly." It quoted one girl as saying: "This is my country but after the way we have been treated I hope never to see it again. . . . As long as my father was working and spending his money in Gary stores, paying taxes, and supporting us, it was all right, but now we have found we can't get justice here." Other families informed the Institute that they had been cut from welfare rolls for refusing to participate in the repatriation program. As Joseph Alimillo, then a teenager who was repatriated, put it, many Mexicans were "forced" into repatriation while others because of the language barrier and fear of government were "sort of fooled into it."[28]

In January 1933 the Institute optimistically discerned a change in the policies of the township trustees. The investigator who refused to aid unwilling deportees resigned. It seemed discrimination had ended, since the township office reinstated several Mexican families previously stricken from relief rolls. Although this major grievance seemed rectified, petty harassment of unemployed Mexicans continued. A Mexican relief applicant reported to the Institute that a welfare investigator demanded surrender of his "first papers" (for citizenship) when he refused to return to Mexico. This unemployed worker had lived in the United States many years and had married an American woman.[29]

Job discrimination continued against remaining Mexicans. From May to September 1933, the steel corporations demanded that workers produce citizenship papers, or at least "first papers," to continue holding jobs in the mills. (This requirement affected Mexicans severely, since most had not become naturalized citizens). During the mid-1930s Mexican aliens were denied W.P.A. work. In Gary, the *Post-Tribune* strongly promoted this policy. After reporting that about three hundred Gary aliens would lose W.P.A. jobs, it argued that "it's high time the W.P.A. payrolls were purged." Whenever men are hired, the *Post-Tribune* said, they should be asked "Are you a citizen?" It added that "the mills are requiring

28 Elizabeth N. Wilson, "Notes on the Early History of the International Institute of Gary," I.I. Papers; Monthly Report, Sept. 1932, *ibid.*; interview with Joseph Alimillo, Gary, Indiana, Aug. 1970.

29 Monthly Reports, Jan. 1933, Feb. 1934, I.I. Papers. "First papers" are those obtained by an immigrant on officially filing his intention to become naturalized. Philip Davis, ed., *Immigration and Americanization* (Boston, 1920), 602–603.

proof of citizenship as a prerequisite to a job. This policy may be extended to all business concerns in Gary." Thus, by mid-1932 voluntary repatriation became forced expulsion, followed by harassment and discrimination against remaining Mexicans.[30]

Mexicans who rejected repatriation did so for various reasons. Many had Americanized children; some had married American citizens. Undoubtedly, many felt too old to start a new life and learn (or relearn) different skills. Others heard of the rigors of both the trip south and the delay before resettlement. The land and jobs promised by the Mexican government never materialized for most repatriates. Moreover, poor conditions prevailed in Juárez, the repatriation depot. As early as 1931 the *New York Times* reported that "many tragic accounts have reached here regarding conditions of the repatriate groups." It mentioned a report that "twenty-six Mexicans died in Ciudad Juárez recently from pneumonia and exposure." The repatriates in Juárez were insufficiently clothed and so crowded that as many as 2,000 lived in a large open corral. When it rained they crowded into customs house examination rooms. The *Survey*, a contemporary magazine devoted to social welfare, described women who "swarmed about the warehouses picking up one by one the beans which spilled through holes in the sacks." Although the *Gary Post-Tribune* did not publicize such conditions, Gary Mexicans knew of the difficulties of repatriation through correspondence with friends who had returned. Also, many, especially single men, who had been repatriated and could find no work returned to Gary almost immediately. They described not only the hardships of the trip, but also the lack of opportunity in Mexico.[31]

The intentions of the Mexican government simply went unfulfilled. Although General Juan José Rios, the Minister of Interior, called on Mexican employers "to do their utmost to find work for those returned," his appeals seemed to have little effect; jobs remained scarce. In fact, the repatriates may even have faced discrimination in Mexico. One American employer in Mexico, asked by

30 *Gary Post-Tribune*, Sept. 8, 1937, p. 22; Monthly Report, May 1933, I.I. Papers; see also Burma, *Spanish-Speaking Groups in the United States*, 70; Robert N. McLean, "The Mexican Return," *Nation*, CXXXV (Aug. 24, 1932), 165–166; Humphrey, "Mexican Repatriation from Michigan," 497–513.

31 *New York Times*, Dec. 8, 1931, p. 22; McLean, "Goodbye Vicente!" 183; Monthly Report, Sept. 1931, I.I. Papers.

an interviewer if he hired many repatriates, answered: "I don't like to employ them once they have been there [to the United States]. They get too smart. . . . They talk to the other workmen and spoil them."[32] Land made available by the Mexican government seldom came with enough water to support even subsistence agriculture. Because of such difficulties, most repatriates returned to the country's villages and small towns. Sociologist Emory S. Bogardus suggested that eighty percent returned to the villages because "only the most resourceful are able to get readjusted in the large cities within a reasonable length of time." He contended that another fifteen percent went to larger cities and only five percent to repatriation settlements. Similarly, James Gilbert, a graduate student at the University of Southern California who made a field study of Mexican repatriation, found that approximately twenty-five percent went to cities of ten thousand or more, while the remainder returned to the villages where they lived before migrating to the United States. Those who chose another place to live invariably selected a town larger than the one in which they had been raised. Very few ended up in new agricultural settlements. Thus, a haven in the homeland did not materialize for the repatriates—victims of depression and discrimination in the United States.[33]

Mexicans had migrated to Gary for the same reasons that other immigrants had come—to make a better life for themselves. But, as all unskilled migrants to industrial cities discovered, the good life was elusive. Although in the 1920s Gary's steel workers, including unskilled Mexicans, could count on fairly steady employment, the depression shattered the city's economy. There was little work as local business shut down. Even U. S. Steel operated at only ten percent of capacity during 1932 and seldom at much more than fifty percent during the remainder of the depression. The city itself faced financial collapse. Local government, like other depositors, lost funds placed in the city banks. Only one Gary bank, the U. S. Steel-controlled Gary State Bank, did not collapse. Simultaneously, tax revenues dwindled; city and county governments complained

---

[32] *New York Times*, July 9, 1932, p. 7; Emma R. Stevenson, "The Emigrant Comes Home," *Survey*, LXVI (May 1, 1931), 177.

[33] Bogardus, "Mexican Repatriates," 170–174; James Carl Gilbert, "A Field Study in Mexico of the Mexican Repatriation Movement" (M.A. thesis, University of Southern California, 1934), 32–33.

of tax delinquencies that reached twenty-five percent annually. In the face of these setbacks, relief costs seemed staggering. With the local press depicting Mexicans as perennially unemployed, and national publications representing Mexicans as lazy and unassimilable, the traditional Gary anti-Mexican attitude intensified. "Unofficial deportation," to use the realistic words of the *Gary Post-Tribune*, became acceptable—even virtuous—to the city at large.

The poverty, discrimination, and repatriation of Gary's Mexicans illustrates an unexplored part of Mexican-American history. The inequity and intolerance confronting Mexican immigrants typified hostilities directed against all aliens in depression America. The tensions generated by economic breakdown renewed the nativism of the 1920s. The deportations of aliens in general, and the repatriation of Mexicans in particular, revealed the xenophobia of American society during the early years of the Great Depression.

"Mexican American" and "Chicano": Emerging Terms for a People Coming of Age

Richard L. Nostrand

The author is a member of the geography department in the University of Oklahoma.

Some years ago while conversing with a local resident in Las Vegas, New Mexico, I absent-mindedly inquired whether this individual were a "Mexican American." He bristled, replying that no, he was a "Spanish American." For me, this experience underscored a phenomenon which characterizes people of Spanish-Indian or Mexican descent: the existence of regional variations in self-reference terms.

"Spanish American" (sometimes simply "Spanish") and "Mexican American," together with "Latin American" (sometimes "Latin"), "Chicano(-a)," and "Mexican," are terms having the greatest currency in the American Southwest where members of this sizable minority are concentrated.[1] They are the important terms by which "Hispanos" (used in this paper as an all-inclusive label) refer to themselves collectively.[2] But, with the exception of Chicano, they are used by Hispanos only when speaking in English; when speaking in Spanish, *mexicano* is most prevalent, although one also hears

---

[1] Several terms of lesser currency include "Spanish-speaking," "Spanish surname," "Spanish Colonial," "native," and "Hispano."

[2] Indeed, they are also used by "Anglos" (as members of the numerically dominant group in the Southwest are called) when referring to Hispanos, but so, too, are other terms—including the pejorative "meskin," "greaser," and "spic," for example.

raza or la raza (literally, "the race," but figuratively, "the [our] people").[3]

That these different self-referents exist is recognized in much of the literature concerning this minority,[4] but there has been no attempt to synthesize this information in one place or to go beyond it and indicate which terms are currently in greater use and where. What follows is an attempt to do so,[5] a task that must take into account certain historical patterns.

Spanish-Mexican colonization of the Southwest was not, of course, the result of one grand march to the north but of lesser enterprises separated in time and space on a distant frontier.[6] Earliest

---

[3] Arthur Campa noted that when the native New Mexican uses the word *mexicano* he does not mean "Mexican," but rather is referring to "a concept of culture that no other term, not even a translation of that same term, can convey." Arthur L. Campa, *Spanish Folk-Poetry in New Mexico* (Albuquerque, 1946), 16. Other terms are used when speaking in Spanish, but they are usually associated with a relatively small geographic area. For example, *latino* is an important self-referent in San Antonio. Leo Grebler *et al.*, *The Mexican-American People: The Nation's Second Largest Minority* (New York, 1970), 386–387. And native New Mexicans refer to each other as *manitos*, a term derived from their custom of affectionately calling one another *hermanito* (little brother). Donovan Senter and Florence Hawley, "The Grammar School as the Basic Acculturating Influence for Native New Mexicans," *Social Forces*, XXIV (1945–46), 398.

[4] The more lengthy discussions of these terms are those found in Campa, *Spanish Folk-Poetry in New Mexico*, 12–16; Erna Fergusson, *New Mexico: A Pageant of Three Peoples* (New York, 1951), 217–218; Manuel Gamio, *Mexican Immigration to the United States: A Study of Human Migration and Adjustment* (Chicago, 1930), 129, 130, 133, 209, 210, 233; Grebler *et al.*, *The Mexican-American People*, 385–387; Nancie L. González, *The Spanish Americans of New Mexico: A Distinctive Heritage* (Los Angeles, 1967), 58, 126, 129–130; Clark S. Knowlton, "Cultural Factors in the Non-Delivery of Medical Services to Southwestern Mexican Americans," in American Association for the Advancement of Science, Committee on Desert and Arid Zone Research Symposium, *Health Related Problems in Arid Lands*, edited by M. S. Riedesel (Tempe, 1971), Contribution No. 14, pp. 61–62; Carey McWilliams, *North from Mexico: The Spanish-Speaking People of the United States* (Philadelphia, 1949), 78–79, 102, 209; Leonard Pitt, *The Decline of the Californios: A Social History of the Spanish-Speaking Californians, 1846–1890* (Berkeley and Los Angeles, 1966), 7, 309–310; and Daniel T. Valdes and Tom Pino, *Ethnic Labels in Majority-Minority Relations* (Denver, 1968 [reprinted from the Denver *Post*]).

[5] It is beyond the scope of this paper to differentiate among the several self-referents by socio-economic class, although one question asked on the questionnaire (footnote 43 below) and during interviews concerned precisely this. Several comments regarding class differences are made where it seems pertinent to do so. For data on variations in self-referents by socio-economic class, see Grebler *et al.*, *The Mexican-American People*, 385–387, 583.

[6] The standard work on this colonization has been Herbert E. Bolton's seminal *The Spanish Borderlands: A Chronicle of Old Florida and the Southwest* (New Haven, 1921), a synthesis of the author's own research over the preceding two decades, and of the research of others. John Francis Bannon has again synthesized the now consider-

colonization occurred in the upper Río Grande Valley of Nuevo México, the result of a private venture led by Juan de Oñate in 1598 (Fig. 1). A century elapsed before missions began to be built

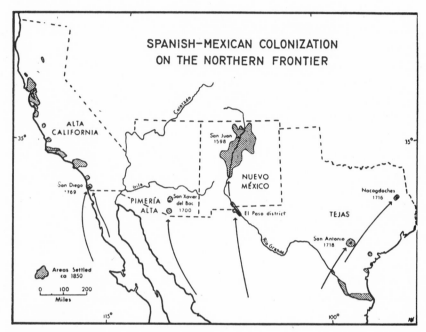

FIGURE 1. Spanish-Mexican Colonization on the Northern Frontier, ca. 1850.

(the first in 1700) in a second area of the present-day Southwest, northern Pimería Alta. In a score of years several settlements had been founded in Tejas (the earlier settled El Paso district was considered part of Nuevo México until the nineteenth century), and beginning in 1769 colonists converged by land and sea on Alta California. By the time of the signing of the Treaty of Guadalupe Hidalgo (1848) and the purchase of land by James Gadsden (1853) —events marking the frontier's transition to United States political status—settlements were numerous and widespread and the Mexican population numbered over 80,000.[7]

able literature on the Borderlands in his *The Spanish Borderlands Frontier, 1513–1821* (New York, 1970).

[7] Richard L. Nostrand, "The Hispanic-American Borderland: Delimitation of an American Culture Region," *Annals of the Association of American Geographers,* LX (1970), 646–647.

Of the 80,000 Mexicans three-fourths lived in the basin of the upper Río Grande, an area made even more distinctive by certain cultural attributes. When the region was settled, some colonists practiced self-flagellation and other rites of the Penitente Brotherhood (introduced with Juan de Oñate, himself a Penitente), and all spoke Spanish. Some of these practices and certain features of this now archaic speech were perpetuated by New Mexicans in their isolation from others.[8] Also perpetuated were the folk songs and plays brought from Iberia and transmitted orally from generation to generation. There developed an indigenous art form in which depictions of Christian saints (santos) were carved and painted—a craft which flourished in the first quarter of the nineteenth century.[9] Thus, a folk culture with roots deep in the Spanish era was already in existence in New Mexico by the mid-nineteenth century.

Following the American takeover of the Southwest in 1848, Hispanic patterns underwent significant modification. One change resulted from the internal migration of those already residing in the Southwest, notably the movement of New Mexicans into south central Colorado (Fig. 2).[10] A second resulted from the in-migration of Mexicans who reinforced numbers in existing settlements, or settled in new areas. From a trickle in the nineteenth century, the influx of migrants grew to a flood in the twentieth century, nearly 500,000 arriving during the 1920s alone. The two states receiving the largest numbers were Texas and California; Arizona received far fewer, and, by comparison, New Mexico and Colorado practically none.[11] A third change resulted from the arrival in the Southwest of non-Hispanos. Even before the American period the number of

---

[8] Erna Fergusson stated that Juan de Oñate was a Penitente in her *New Mexico*, 153; Charles F. Lumis, *The Land of Poco Tiempo* (New York, 1897), chap. 4; Aurelio M. Espinosa noted some "archaic words and expressions, constructions and sounds" used by New Mexicans in his *The Spanish Language in New Mexico and Southern Colorado* (Santa Fe, 1911), 8–9.

[9] Russell V. Hunter, "Latin-American Art in U. S. A.," *Design*, XLIV, No. 7 (1942–43), 20.

[10] Francis T. Cheetham discussed the ephemeral or relatively unsuccessful attempts to colonize southern Colorado in the 1830s and 1840s. See his "The Early Settlements of Southern Colorado," *Colorado Magazine*, V (1928), 4–5. San Luis, founded in 1851, is acknowledged to be Colorado's earliest permanent settlement. See LeRoy R. Hafen, "Colorado Cities—Their Founding and the Origin of Their Names," *Colorado Magazine*, IX (1932), 182.

[11] Leo Grebler *et al.*, *Mexican Immigration to the United States: The Record and Its Implications* (Los Angeles, 1966), Tables 1 and 2; see also pp. 51–56.

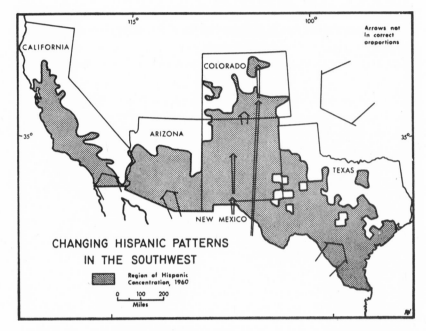

FIGURE 2. Changing Hispanic Patterns in the Southwest, 1850–1960.

easterners and others who had gone to Texas and California was sufficient to engulf the resident Mexicans. Thereafter, numbers continued to swell and Hispanos were put increasingly in the minority.

By 1970 nearly 6,200,000 Hispanos (17.1 percent of the total population) inhabited the five southwestern states.[12] An additional contingent, nearly 3,100,000 in size, had found its way to the non-southwestern states,[13] but these Hispanos were widely scattered, many living in cities of the Middle West (notably Chicago). Thus, of the 9,300,000, two-thirds resided in the Southwest, the prepon-

---

12 U. S. **Bureau of the Census**, *Census of Population: 1970 General Social and Economic Characteristics,* Final report PC(1)–C (Washington, D. C., 1971), Table 49. Being identified were all persons (except Puerto Ricans who were identified separately) of Spanish surname or whose mother tongue was Spanish; these persons were largely of Mexican descent.

13 U. S. **Bureau of the Census**, *Census of Population: 1970 General Social and Economic Characteristics,* Final Report PC(1)–C1 United States Summary (Washington, D.C., 1972), Table 86. This figure was derived by subtracting the 6,200,000 Hispanos in the Southwest from the nearly 9,300,000 persons of Spanish heritage (persons, exclusive of Puerto Ricans, whose mother tongue was Spanish or who possess Spanish surnames) given in Table 86 for the entire United States.

derance within the region delimited (Fig. 2).[14] With over four-fifths of the southwestern Hispanic population in Texas and California, the pattern in 1970 was one heavily weighted to either end of the region—a complete reversal from that of a century before when three-fourths of the Mexicans lived in the region's center.

This is a distinctive yet highly diverse minority which is heavily concentrated in the more southerly Southwest. Most Hispanos are mestizo, yet some trace their lineage to Spaniards (as do certain New Mexicans), perhaps others to Indians. Most speak Spanish as a mother tongue,[15] yet a few speak English in the home. Most are disadvantaged socio-economically, yet there are those who have advanced to a higher status. Over eighty-two percent are native-born and are, therefore, United States citizens, while of the remaining foreign-born only a small percentage have become naturalized citizens.[16] There are, of course, vast differences in how far back the native-born can trace their ancestry in the United States—most not very far. Out of this diverse background sprang the several self-referents.

During the years of Spanish and Mexican political rule, the inhabitants of the northern frontier referred to themselves quite appropriately as "Spaniards" (*españoles*) and "Mexicans" (*mexicanos*). "Spaniard" did not abruptly disappear after 1821. Lewis Garrard, when traveling to Taos in 1846–1847, found it a "common term" (if one can infer that what native New Mexicans were called reflected what they called themselves).[17] On the other hand, "Mex-

14 To be included within this region (which is based on 1960 census data), counties or parts thereof had to meet minimum absolute and relative values established for determining Hispanic populations of greater relative importance. See Nostrand, "The Hispanic-American Borderland," 655–658.

15 On the persistence of Spanish within the minority, see Grebler *et al.*, *The Mexican-American People*, 423–428.

16 The native-born percentage is calculated from U. S. Bureau of the Census, *Census of Population: 1970 General Social and Economic Characteristics*, Final Report PC(1)–C, Table 49. Naturalization data are given in Ralph Guzmán, "Politics and Policies of the Mexican-American Community," in Eugene P. Dvorin and Arthur J. Misner, eds., *California Politics and Policies* (Palo Alto, 1966), 366.

17 "Spaniard" was used, Garrard explained, because "they speak the Spanish language." Lewis H. Garrard, *Wah-To-Yah and the Taos Trail* (New York, 1850), 181. Antonio Barreiro noted in his "glance" over New Mexico written in 1831–1832 that the Pueblo Indians referred to the Hispanos as "Spaniards." Lansing B. Bloom, ed., "Barreiro's Ojeada Sobre Nuevo-Mexico," *New Mexico Historical Review*, III (1928), 88.

ican" increased in currency; it was the term Garrard usually used, and it was apparently prevalent everywhere on the frontier except in California.[18] There, feelings of patriotism were "vague and contradictory," and to show autonomy within the Mexican Republic, natives referred to themselves as "Californios."[19]

After the Mexican War native New Mexicans continued to refer to themselves as "Mexicans," but contempt for Mexicans was widespread among Anglos who used the term disparagingly.[20] Under these circumstances, it is perhaps surprising that "Mexican" prevailed as long as it did. For, according to Erna Fergusson, it was not until World War I that "Spanish-American" was "invented" in New Mexico by those who wished to praise the readiness of natives to fight but who lacked a term for doing so.[21] This diplomatic label rapidly caught on among Hispanos (also Anglos) in the 1920s.[22] Significantly, this was precisely the time when relatively large numbers of Mexican immigrants were arriving—a group which the natives wished to disassociate themselves from in part because of its generally lower socio-economic status.[23] By "Spanish American" a

---

18 Although seemingly not prevalent, *"tejano"* was apparently used in Texas as a self-referent among the native-born, especially those of the upper socio-economic class. See Emory S. Bogardus, *The Mexican in the United States* (Los Angeles, 1934), 9, citing Lee C. Harby, "Texan Types and Contrasts," *Harper's Magazine*, LXXXI (1890), 229–246—apparently by mistake, for Harby does not mention *tejano*; see also McWilliams, *North from Mexico*, 102.

19 Pitt, *The Decline of the Californios*, 7, 25.

20 The use of "Mexican" occurred at least as early as 1841 when, according to Ruth Barker, Texans of the Texan-Santa Fe Expedition "used the term 'Mexican' with insulting ridicule" while in New Mexico. Ruth L. Barker, "Where Americans are 'Anglos,'" *North American Review*, CCXXVIII (1929), 569.

21 Fergusson, *New Mexico*, 217–218. "Spanish American" was not unknown prior to World War I. Writing in 1856, Francisco P. Ramirez, editor of *El Clamor Público* in Los Angeles, used it when referring to people of Mexican descent. Pitt, *The Decline of the Californios*, 181. Mary Austin noted that it was about World War I that "Spanish-Colonial" came into use. Mary Austin, "Mexicans and New Mexico," *Survey Graphic*, LXVI (1931), 142–143.

22 Erna Fergusson, "New Mexico's Mexicans," *Century Magazine*, CXVI (1928), 437; Helen Zunser, "A New Mexican Village," *Journal of American Folklore*, XLVIII (1935), 141. Interestingly, literary writers did not foster the acceptance of the term "Spanish American" among Anglos. For example, Erna Fergusson used "Mexican" and made a point of her preference for it in "New Mexico's Mexicans," 437–438. In her "Mexicans and New Mexico," Mary Austin used "native," "Spanish speaking," "Spanish-Indian people," and "Spanish-Colonial" (pp. 142, 144, 188, 189, and 190), but not "Spanish-American," a term that, in her opinion, native New Mexicans did not like (p. 142).

23 Manuel Gamio, *Mexican Immigration to the United States*, 129, 209; Zunser, "A

native meant that he was native-born of *Spanish* descent—a claim which could be made with justification if a Spanish-derived folk culture were being implied, but not if it implied a direct Spanish lineage, since most natives were mestizo.[24]

After the Mexican War discrimination against persons of Mexican descent became especially severe in Texas (also in "Little Texas," an area in southeastern New Mexico). There, the southerner's attitude toward Negroes was carried over to the less dark Mexican, and the word "Mexican" was used with hatred.[25] Presumably some Hispanos—like the small number of descendants of early colonists at Nacogdoches today—referred to themselves as "Spanish," still others as *tejanos,* but most called themselves "Mexicans." Thus, when "Latin American" was coined, it was probably welcomed. Just how and when this took place is not clear. It was apparently in use in south Texas prior to the founding there in 1929 of LULAC, the League of United Latin American Citizens, for that organization was formed from a merger of three organizations, one of which was the League of Latin American Citizens.[26] This polite term did not become widespread in Texas until after World War II, however. With certain exceptions,[27] the Hispano, when referring to himself as a "Latin American," meant that he was native-born of Mexican descent. But the educated who use this term are aware of its broader meaning to include most people of the Western Hemisphere south of the Río Grande.

Self-referents evolved somewhat differently in California. There,

New Mexican Village," 141. Regarding this notion that the native-born wished to avoid "Mexican" because of the opprobrium attached to it by Anglos, see McWilliams, *North from Mexico,* 79, 209, and González, *The Spanish Americans of New Mexico,* 58, 126, 130.

24 Regarding these confused notions of race, see Campa, *Spanish Folk-Poetry in New Mexico,* 12–13.

25 R. L. Chambers, "The New Mexico Pattern," *Common Ground,* IX (Summer 1949), 20–27; Evon Z. Vogt, "American Subcultural Continua as Exemplified by the Mormons and Texans," *American Anthropologist,* LVII (1955), 1169–1170; Gamio, *Mexican Immigration to the United States,* 210.

26 Edward D. Garza, "LULAC (League of United Latin American Citizens)" (M.A. thesis, Southwest Texas State Teachers College, San Marcos, 1951), chap. 2. George I. Sánchez, late professor of Latin American education at the University of Texas, Austin, suggested that Alonso S. Perales, a founder of LULAC and a resident of San Antonio, may have been the inventor of the term. Personal correspondence, Sept. 29, 1969.

27 For example, one born in Mexico but who had lived many years in Texas might refer to himself as a "Latin American."

the term "Californio" persisted among the native-born until the 1880s. Meanwhile, people calling themselves "Mexicans" were arriving from Mexico, and Californios, especially those of the upper class, behaved with animosity towards these foreign-born. In turn, both the Californio and the Mexican were alienated by the Anglo who considered each to be inferior because he was part Indian.[28] Perhaps it was this situation that prompted the Californios to refer to themselves increasingly as "Spanish"—apparently to emphasize their Spanish descent[29]—in an attempt to disassociate themselves from "Mexicans" in the eyes of Anglos. So important did "Spanish" become that, by the early twentieth century at San Fernando, even those born in Mexico were calling themselves "Spanish," and for an Anglo to use "Mexican" meant he had a fight on his hands.[30] Just how widespread the use of "Spanish" among the foreign-born became is not clear, and today only a small number of Californio descendants, notably those at Santa Barbara and at other nearby places where they were in the majority for some time, refer to themselves as "Spanish."[31]

"Mexican" was apparently the prevalent self-referent among the California-bound immigrants of the 1920s, but the term which eventually prevailed among their descendants was "Mexican American." One wonders where and when this term originated. Its use predates the Second World War after which it became prevalent in California,[32] for there is evidence that it was being applied as early as 1930 to south Texas American citizens of Mexican descent.[33] What one meant when using this term, of course, was that he was native-born of Mexican descent.

---

28 Pitt, *The Decline of the Californios,* 309, 53, 157, 174, 188, 204, 259, 267.

29 "Apparently" is well chosen, for Pitt stated that, when the Californio used "Spaniard," he gave it the connotation of "Spanish-speaking" (*ibid.*, 310). If this were the case, however, one wonders why, "to this day, the dons' descendants refuse to acknowledge their mestizo ancestry or to recognize that their grandfathers acquired Mexican, not Spanish, land grants" (*ibid.*, 290).

30 Interview with Joseph E. Spencer, professor of geography at the University of California, Los Angeles, Aug. 27, 1969. As a youth, Spencer attended the Westside School in San Fernando.

31 This use of "Spanish" was reported on questionnaires returned by Hispanos in the Santa Barbara area. Data gathered by means of questionnaires are discussed below in conjunction with the distribution of self-referents.

32 Many Hispanos who responded to questionnaires in California noted that "Mexican American" became prevalent there only after World War II.

33 O. Douglas Weeks, "The Texas-Mexican and the Politics of South Texas," *American Political Science Review,* XXIV (1930), 617–618.

Perhaps even older than "Mexican American" is "Chicano." There is record of this term having been used in a Spanish-language newspaper in Laredo as early as 1911 to differentiate between a person of Mexican descent who had not been "Americanized" (the "chicano") and another who had.[34] This term, or at least one similar to it, was also in use about 1930 when Manuel Gamio noted that immigrants from Mexico were often derogatorily referred to by the native-born as "chicamos" (spelled with an "m" rather than an "n").[35] "Chicano" was also used in the 1930s as a term of endearment among Hispanos.[36] When used in these ways, the word, which in derivation is probably a dialectal form of "xicano" (from *mexicano*), was confined during these early years to the minority when speaking only in Spanish.[37]

These usages limited only to Spanish have been greatly overshadowed by a more recent development. About the mid-1960s younger and more militant minority members who were inspired by the black civil rights movement of the preceding decade began to demand their equal rights and to organize politically to solve their social and economic problems. Like the blacks, they rejected the strategy of earlier generations which was to assimilate with the majority, and they acquired a new sense of pride in their heritage which led them to demand bilingual and bicultural educational programs and self-study centers in colleges and universities. These minority members seized upon "Chicano" as a self-referent when speaking in English or Spanish, a phenomenon which one might speculate happened first in California where "Chicano" is most prevalent.[38] A "Chicano," then, was someone (of Mexican de-

---

34 "Vicios de Raza," *La Crónica* (Laredo), July 27, 1911, p. 3. José E. Limón, acting director of the Center of Mexican-American Studies at the University of Texas, Austin, pointed this out to me in August 1972.

35 Gamio, *Mexican Immigration to the United States*, 129.

36 In this context, Carlos A. Rojas, professor emeritus of foreign languages at Fresno State College, believes Chicano stemmed from *chico* which means "young one" or "small one." Personal correspondence, July 22, 1969.

37 Several informants, including Thomas M. Pearce, professor emeritus of English at the University of New Mexico, suggested this derivation. Personal correspondence, May 6, 1969. See also Gamio, *Mexican Immigration to the United States*, 233. That Chicano was initially confined to use only within the minority is noted by Celia S. Heller, "Chicano is Beautiful," *Commonweal*, XCI (1969–70), 456.

38 Alfredo Cuéllar's belief that the Chicano movement originated in southern California (in 1966) supports the assumption that it was in California that "Chicano" was first adopted as a self-referent when speaking in English. Alfredo Cuéllar, "Perspective on Politics," in Joan W. Moore, *Mexican Americans* (Englewood Cliffs, N.J.,

scent) who identified with a new, aggressive, highly self-conscious subculture—a subculture separate from either that of the Anglo from whom the Chicano felt alienated or that of the Mexican from whom the Chicano had grown apart. Many older Hispanos resent this "slang" use of Chicano, as they call it, and are apprehensive about the Chicano movement itself.[39]

Curiously, in Arizona and eastern Colorado no term seems to have replaced "Mexican."[40] The relative recency with which Mexicans first settled in eastern Colorado[41] (New Mexicans had colonized areas further west) is perhaps one reason why no term replaced "Mexican" in that area, but such cannot be said of Arizona. There (as indeed everywhere), persons of Mexican descent were discriminated against and "Mexican" was used derisively. Also, the native-born citizens began to outnumber the Mexican-born aliens in the decades after the large immigrant influx of the 1920s with the result that referring to oneself as a "Mexican" was no longer appropriate for the majority. Even so, "Mexican" persisted, although Anglos in time used it with less invective, the degree of their reproach depending on how they said the word. Thus, in two areas "Mexican" took on a double meaning; on the one hand, it embraced those who were Mexican-born and noncitizens—*everywhere* in the Southwest people of this status so refer to themselves[42]—while, on the other hand,

---

1970), 149. That "Chicano" is today most prevalent in California was established through interviews and from questionnaire respondents; both these sources of data are discussed below in conjunction with the distribution of self-referents.

[39] That many older Hispanos were opposed to this use of "Chicano" was determined from interviews, and the data provided by questionnaire respondents concurred in this regard. Regarding the Chicano movement, see Grebler *et al.*, *The Mexican-American People*, 553–554.

[40] In Arizona, however, some native-born did prefer "Spanish." For example, Gamio noted that the Spanish-American Alliance, founded in Tucson in the late nineteenth century, adopted the word so as not to "wound the sensibilities" of those of Spanish origin. Gamio, *Mexican Immigration to the United States*, 133.

[41] Mexicans began arriving in the South Platte and Arkansas river valleys sometime after sugar beets were introduced about 1900; they gradually replaced German-Russian and Japanese field workers, supplying most of the labor by the 1920s and 1930s. See Colin B. Goodykoontz, "The People of Colorado," in LeRoy R. Hafen, ed., *Colorado and Its People: A Narrative and Topical History of the Centennial State* (New York, 1948), II, 100; W.P.A. Writers' Program, *Colorado: A Guide to the Highest State* (New York, 1941), 65–66, 165.

[42] That Mexican aliens everywhere refer to themselves as "Mexicans" was determined through interviews and from questionnaire respondents. However, Nancie González noted that in New Mexico Spanish Americans of the middle and upper classes refer to Spanish Americans of the lower class as "Mexicans"; in this context, "Mexican" does not mean one born in Mexico and a noncitizen. González, *The Spanish Americans of New Mexico*, 129–130.

it included those who were native-born and of Mexican descent.

In most of the Southwest during the present century, then, several terms came to replace "Mexican" among the native-born of Mexican descent. Several reasons for this have already been suggested in the preceding discussion. In addition, certain regional differences in the Southwest suggest why given terms arose where they did. In New Mexico, for example, relatively large numbers of Spaniards colonized early, and their descendants could look with pride to their Spanish-derived folk culture. "Spanish American" seemed an appropriate choice. On the other hand, in Texas and California (and even in Arizona), tendencies on the part of the native-born upper socio-economic class to refer to itself as "Spanish" during the nineteenth century were suppressed, for, unlike New Mexico, the number of native-born in these two areas was relatively small, and those present were engulfed by the immigrants. "Latin American" and "Mexican American" were, of course, the terms adopted. "Spanish American" and "Latin American," unlike "Mexican American," are euphemisms. Perhaps a euphemism was less needed in California where "Mexican American" took hold. Discrimination (and the correlated enmity with which "Mexican" was used) was certainly less severe there than in Texas and southeastern New Mexico. "Mexican American" seemed appropriate in California.

Thus, for various reasons Hispanic subgroups came to designate themselves by one of several terms, and within the region of Hispanic concentration, there exists today a distinct pattern of regional usage (Fig. 3). For purposes of delimiting these present regions, questionnaires were sent out and interviews were conducted. Data gathered from Hispanos in these ways are summarized in Table 1.

In order to gain an initial impression of the regional usage of the several self-referents, 395 questionnaires were sent to managers of chambers of commerce within the study area in the spring and early summer of 1969. Sending questionnaires to chamber of commerce managers had the advantage of securing quickly and inexpensively a relatively large body of data spread evenly throughout the study area. The disadvantage was that these data would be supplied by non-Hispanos. However, I reasoned that even non-Hispanos could tell me what the *prevailing* local self-referent was among His-

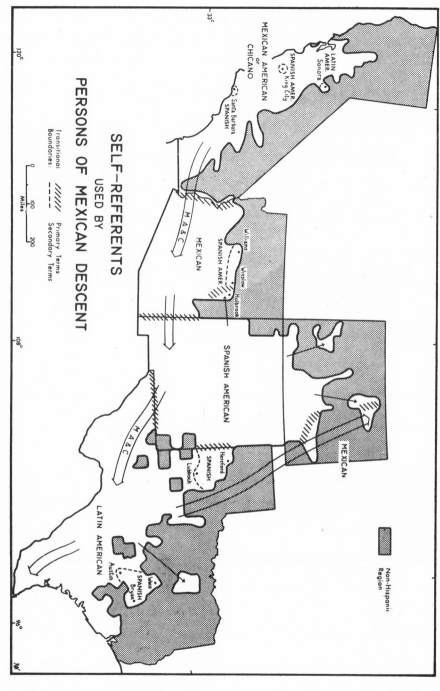

FIGURE 3. Self-Referents used by Persons of Mexican Descent, 1969-1972. SOURCE: data in Table 1.

TABLE 1. SELF-REFERENTS IN ENGLISH PREVAILING AMONG AMERICANS OF MEXICAN DESCENT ("HISPANOS") IN THE REGION OF HISPANIC CONCENTRATION, 1969–1972

State	Mexican	Mexican Americana	Chicano(-a)a	Spanish or Spanish Americanb	Latin or Latin American	Total
Arizona	9	4	3	2		18
California	5	32	23	2		62
Colorado	2	1	1	7		11
New Mexico				6		6
Texas		21	4	4	32	61
Total	16	58	31	21	32	158

SOURCE: Data compiled from 59 interviews with Hispanos and 99 questionnaires returned by Hispanos between 1969–1972.

a Respondents in Arizona, Colorado, and Texas noted that "Mexican American" began to be used about the early 1960s, and that "Chicano" began to be used in the latter 1960s. "Chicano" is also a self-referent when speaking in Spanish. The seemingly low scores for "Chicano" in California and Texas are explained by the fact that 20 Hispanos who gave "Mexican American" as the prevailing term among most minority members and "Chicano" as the prevailing term among younger minority members were all recorded as favoring "Mexican American."

b The relatively low number of Hispanos who reported "Spanish" or "Spanish American" in New Mexico merely reflects the fact that few Hispanos in that state chose to return questionnaires.

panos.[43] I further requested that the chamber of commerce managers furnish me with names of Hispanos who might respond to the same questionnaire. In all, 295 questionnaires were returned, 46 from Hispanos, who, because they were acquaintances of the chamber of commerce managers, represented largely the "establishment" portion of their respective communities.

There were obvious places for which the data were conflicting or questionable, and these places were visited during August 1969. At that time 66 additional persons, 43 of them Hispanos, were interviewed in 39 communities located in central Texas, west Texas, eastern Colorado, central New Mexico, north central Arizona, and central California. The approach taken in the field was usually to go to the priest or minister of the local church (about one out of four of these clergymen was of Mexican descent), explain the study to him, and ask for the names of community residents of Mexican

43 This was the principal question to which an answer was desired. Other questions concerned the length of time the prevailing term had been used, whether a term preference existed among those of different socio-economic classes, and the term or terms used by non-Hispanic people when referring to Hispanic people. An accompanying letter identified the group referred to as "Hispanic."

descent. A conscious effort was made to interview persons from the several socio-economic strata, although in those cases where persons interviewed had been referred to me by a member of the clergy, I was, of course, sampling only from among church members. In these interviews (as in the questionnaires), the principal purpose was to determine which self-referent prevailed locally. This was not necessarily the self-referent the individual himself may have preferred.

An additional 16 Hispanos were interviewed during the summer of 1971 while I was teaching at the University of Arizona, and during the 1971–1972 academic year while I was undertaking research and also teaching at the University of Texas at Austin. These individuals were, for the most part, students, and by and large they represented the young, nonchurch-attending segment of the community.

While in Austin I learned that a directory of Spanish-speaking organizations had been published in July 1970.[44] Drawing heavily on this source for potential respondents, I sent out 175 additional questionnaires in the fall of 1972 to organizations within the study area. This mailing netted 54 returns, 53 of them from Hispanos who represented mainly the middle and upper socio-economic strata. Thus, the distribution which follows is based on interviews with or questionnaires returned by 158 Hispanos from all walks of life.

"Mexican" is, of course, the self-referent of Mexican-born persons. But it is also the *prevailing* self-referent among the native-born in much of Arizona and in eastern Colorado. Why this is so in Arizona remains an enigma. The spatial proximity of those who refer to themselves as "Mexicans" to those who refer to themselves as "Spanish Americans" is perhaps a reason for the persistence of "Mexican" in eastern Colorado, however. For one of Mexico's nationalistic themes after acquiring independence was the emphasis on its Indian ancestry and heritage, a development which led Ruth Barker to quip that it is more insulting to call a Mexican in Mexico a "Spaniard" than it is to call a Spanish American in the United States a "Mexican."[45] Perhaps for this reason, the Mexicans of

---

[44] Cabinet Committee on Opportunity for the Spanish Speaking, *Directory of Spanish Speaking Community Organizations June 1970* (Washington, D.C., 1970).
[45] Barker, "Where Americans are 'Anglos,' " 569.

eastern Colorado, many of whom were descendants of those who had recently come from Mexico, rejected "Spanish American."[46] Another explanation may be found in the fact that they were rather far removed from the areas where the other terms were popular.

"Spanish American," sometimes "Spanish," is the *primary* self-referent in most of New Mexico where its distribution corresponds to a remarkable degree with state boundaries. It is also the *primary* self-referent in places where New Mexicans settled: in south central Colorado and areas farther north in that state, and in eastern Arizona in the vicinity of Show Low, Snowflake, and Holbrook. It is of secondary use (after "Mexican") in the area west of Holbrook, between Winslow and Williams, where New Mexicans are a minority.[47] "Spanish" is also of secondary importance where descendants of "old families" are numerous, for example, at Santa Barbara and nearby Carpinteria in California and at Nacogdoches (located outside the study area) in Texas.

When using "Spanish American" or "Spanish," New Mexicans or the descendants of "old families" mean that they are native-born of Spanish descent. "Spanish," meaning Spanish speaking, is also used by some in the Southwest but only as a secondary term. This is the case in two parts of Texas, one being the area roughly triangular in shape south of Waco and the other being the area between Hereford and Lubbock. (The use of "Spanish" in the latter location is apparently unrelated to the influx of New Mexicans into the region, especially into the larger cities such as Lubbock.) This is also the case in King City, California, where Hispanos refer to themselves as "Spanish Americans," meaning Spanish-speaking. In King City, perhaps also in Texas, schools fostered the terms used.

The *primary* self-referent throughout the Texas part of the region is "Latin American" or "Latin," and, with one exception (of only secondary importance), its use seems to be restricted to Texas. The exception occurs in California's Tuolumne County, in the

---

46 Curiously, when living among those who refer to themselves as "Spanish Americans" in New Mexico (for example, in Albuquerque), middle and upper socioeconomic class descendants of immigrants accept "Spanish American" as a self-referent. González, *The Spanish Americans of New Mexico*, 130.

47 Although not verified in the field, "Spanish American" also appears to be of secondary importance in such southeastern Arizona mining communities as Clifton and Bisbee where New Mexicans are presumably present.

vicinity of Sonora, Tuolumne, and Standard, where a "Latin American Society" composed of persons of Mexican descent and others from Latin American countries has been organized. As a consequence, "Latin American" has become prevalent among "Anglos" in the area when reference is made to persons of Mexican descent, and it is apparently used occasionally by the latter when referring to themselves.

"Mexican American" and "Chicano" are both *primary* terms in the California regional segment, "Mexican American" being prevalent among the majority and "Chicano" among the more militant youth. Unlike the other terms, however, these two are diffusing areally, apparently from their region of greatest usage (arrows shown in Fig. 3 merely suggest apparent areal diffusion from California, and most certainly do not represent paths of movement).[48] Promoted by the press and, with respect to "Chicano," by the rising momentum of the Chicanismo movement, these terms have gained popularity only recently, within the last half dozen years in many areas, but their spread has been rapid. Thus, "Mexican American" and "Chicano" have gained wide use in Arizona, in southern New Mexico (where the descendants of immigrants find them acceptable), and especially in Texas (where in the larger cities and the lower Rio Grande Valley they are preferred by many over "Latin American"). They have also become increasingly popular in the larger cities and agricultural areas of eastern Colorado.[49]

The diffusion of "Mexican American" and "Chicano" portends the possible emergence of a strong sense of a common ethnic identity among Hispanos throughout the Southwest. This development, if successful, may have significant political implications, for it could help provide these peoples with the unity which earlier disagreement over terminology—and what that terminology implied— helped impede. Still, many refuse to change, especially the "Spanish Americans" of New Mexico and southern Colorado, most of whom continue to take umbrage at being called "Mexican Americans."

---

[48] The diffusion of these terms would be a study in itself. Diffusion types (carriers and barriers) and levels in scale (local, regional, and national) are described in Peter R. Gould, "Spatial Diffusion," *Association of American Geographers Commission on College Geography Resource Paper No. 4* (Washington, D.C., 1969).

[49] As noted below, there is also a tendency for younger "Spanish Americans" in New Mexico and Colorado to refer to themselves as "Chicanos."

Because they align themselves with the movement, many younger Hispanos in the region of Spanish American usage are beginning to call themselves "Chicanos," apparently ignoring the pride-in-*Mexican*-heritage connotation attached to this term by most who use it. This development suggests that "Chicano" might appear to be the best hope for a label behind which all Hispanos could unite. It is a term chosen by members of the minority; none construe it as disparaging; and it is not a clumsy combination of terms, hyphenated or otherwise. But it does have its drawbacks, for, unlike "Mexican American," it is not immediately intelligble to many Americans outside the Southwest. Moreover, many Hispanos, especially those who are older, are opposed to its use as a self-referent.

That "Mexican American" and "Chicano" *are* being accepted by many is significant, however, for it indicates that this is a minority coming of age. For those who identify with "Mexican American" and "Chicano" accept, even assert (as in the case with "Chicano") their Mexican heritage. One sees a parallel with America's largest minority: When discrimination was once more overt, Negroes were "niggers" and Mexicans were either that or "meskins." To avoid these opprobrious terms, Negroes turned to "colored," a euphemism analogous to "Spanish American" and "Latin American" to which Hipanos turned. Only recently has the Negro accepted his being "black"—"Black is beautiful," he asserts. With "Mexican American" and "Chicano," so has the person of Mexican descent accepted his being "Mexican." *one way or another*

Index

Index